WHAT THEY'
A BAD CATHOLIC'S ESSAYS ON
WHAT'S WRONG WITH THE WORLD

Looking around at the messy state of our culture, most of us are inclined to think, "Wow, the world really needs Jesus." Fewer of us are inclined to look at that mess and think, "Wow, maybe *I* need Jesus." In *A Bad Catholic's Essays on What's Wrong With the World*, Marc Barnes takes an inventory of the state of society—and more importantly, the state of his own soul—and makes a genuine case that maybe the Church continues to give answers to the problems that ail us all because there's a decent chance those answers might be the right ones.

—**Matt Swaim,** communications coordinator of
The Coming Home Network International,
author of *Prayer in the Digital Age*

What Marc Barnes brings to us with *A Bad Catholic's Essays on What's Wrong With The World* is not just smart words and deep thoughts (though he assuredly brings both), but rather an approach to life that is delightful, unexpected, and true. His essays unpack the important while not forgetting the smiles and laughter that should always accompany them. This collection is a refreshing voice of reason in the midst of a world of turmoil.

—**Sarah Reinhard,**
author and blogger, *SnoringScholar.com*

Although I don't always agree with the author's views, Marc Barnes' writing is always interesting. *A Bad Catholic's Essays on What's Wrong With the World* offers a collection of engaging thought, creative writing, and personal reflection on one Catholic's attempt to make sense of his faith and his world. Whether you are provoked to dispute or affirmed in your views, this book is worth a read.

—Daniel P. Horan, OFM,
author, *God Is Not Fair and Other Reasons for Gratitude*

A Bad Catholic's Essays on What's Wrong With the World

By Marc Barnes

Liguori

Imprimi Potest:
Stephen T. Rehrauer, CSsR, Provincial
Denver Province, the Redemptorists

Published by Liguori Publications
Liguori, Missouri 63057

Liguori Publications, a nonprofit corporation, is an apostolate of
the Redemptorists. To learn more about the Redemptorists, visit
Redemptorists.com

To order, call 800-325-9521 or visit Liguori.org.

Library of Congress Cataloging-in-Publication Data

Names: Barnes, Marc, author.

Title: A bad Catholic's essays on what's wrong with the world / by Marc Barnes.

Identifiers: LCCN 2017041241 | ISBN 9780764827099

Subjects: LCSH: Catholic Church—Doctrines—Blogs. | Christianity and culture—
Blogs. | Theology, Doctrinal—Popular works. | Barnes, Marc—Blogs.

Classification: LCC BX1754 .B3425 2017 | DDC 282—dc23

LC record available at https://lccn.loc.gov/2017041241

Printed in the United States of America * 21 20 19 18 17/5 4 3 2 1 * First Edition
Cover design: Lorena Jimenez * Interior book design: Wendy Barnes
Cover and interior illustrations: NLshop / Shutterstock

DEDICATION

To Brodie Stutzman, remember, Wovenhand in Pittsburgh,
September twenty-first.

Contents

Sex   67

Becoming Catholic   91

INTRODUCTION

Y ou may have picked up this little book after reading my work online. This marks a remarkable occasion. Before, I only wearied your news feed; now, I will weary your shelf. One day we will meet, and I, climbing on your shoulders in a fit of Christian hospitality, will weary your back. Until then, consider this book the partial solidification of my nebulous web presence, and treat me as you would treat any apparition midmaterialization—with patience. Like most apparitions, I have something to say.

You may have picked up this self-same book without an online introduction, as in certain traditional cultures where women meet men without stalking them on Facebook first. If this is the case, I better out myself now. I am a blogger.

Derived from the onomatopoeic prefix *bleaugh*, a blogger is a talentless hack who solves the problem of being unpublishable by getting rid of the publisher. His success is predicated on the stern avoidance of any editors with the authority to call him unsuccessful—like the success of a movie star's foray into hip-hop or a four-year-old's submission of crayon drawings to a refrigerator gallery. Being uninteresting, his career gets its lifeblood by latching onto the already-interesting. No one cares to hear his deep thoughts on the virtue of modesty, so he must wait for a celebrity to be immodest, relying on the already-popular to be popular, on the already-controversial to be controversial. Distressed by this parasitic existence and unable to discern whether he is a commentator or an advertisement for popular culture, the blogger drinks heavily, yells at domesticated animals, and usually ends his career muttering the word *hashtag* at the entrance of a small, sad water park.

AS I VIOLATED COPYRIGHT LAW AFTER COPYRIGHT LAW, I BEGAN TO REALIZE THAT WHAT KEPT THESE WRITERS FRESH AND NEW—BESIDES THEIR EDITORS—WAS THEIR CATHOLICITY.

I was baptized into this new life of unsolicited commentary after reading *Ender's Game* in high school—a 1985 science-fiction novel in which a child beats another child to death and later, having learnt his lesson, beats an alien race to death. Despite an initial appeal, it was not the child beating that inspired me. The author, Orson Scott Card, describes two children who, wishing to take over the world, begin to write on the Net under pseudonymous cloaks. They develop strong, political voices that eventually influence international policies. Soon, the governments of the world are their playthings.

World domination was an inspiring enough prospect to disengage me from my usual hobby of trying to lick off all the cheese of an entire bag of Cheetos, so I started a blog. I called it something grand. I sharpened my political wit.

The difference between the Internet as Card imagined it in 1985 and as it is today can be shown in the rather predictable result of my effort—nobody cared, least of all me. Writing about politics is a little like going to a death metal concert—screaming, then going home and telling your mother you contributed to a meaningful discussion. Whatever two or three comments I culled from whoever it is that comments on the political blogs of American high-schoolers, they were predictably stupid.

The urge to be a gnarly, inflamed, digital wart soon withered. The urge to be a thief blossomed in its place. At the time, I was reading the opposite of what I was writing: Newman, Chesterton, Belloc, C.S. Lewis, Tolkien—a whole host of Catholic and basically Catholic Englishmen who, despite being posted as "passe" by postmodernity, still infect the youth of Athens with hope, joy, and common sense. I didn't know exactly how they did it, only that I wanted to be like them. So I copied them.

As I violated copyright law after copyright law, I began to realize that what kept these writers fresh and new—besides their editors—was their catholicity. They had all latched onto a story that bubbles like a spring underneath a gargantuan mountain of talk; a primary meaning that shoots up like a bottle rocket, explodes, and illuminates the whole landscape of culture and politics for the silly, second-tier conversation that it is. They had all caught a whiff of the breeze blowing from Nazareth. From then on, they wrote, not like commentators, agitators, or empty barrels of wit; not like the politicians and news junkies who make the shallow proclamations of the rich and the powerful into the ultimate bedrock of Public Importance. They wrote like men who had received word of an event of utmost mattering to their neighbors; news of a Fall, a Savior, and the genuine possibility of redemption. They had found that piece of news that does not grow stale with the next news cycle; that story that does not bore upon retelling; that word that shines in the darkness, and the darkness has not overcome it.

I changed my blog name to *BadCatholic*. People tend to ask me why I chose this name and, since I can't remember my reason, I tend to give a different answer to everyone who asks. It's because Catholicism is a religion of people who are very bad

CATHOLICISM IS A RELIGION OF PEOPLE WHO ARE VERY BAD AT THEIR RELIGION.

at their religion. It's because I read it in the subtitle to Walker Percy's *Love in the Ruins*. It's because *Good Catholic* was taken. It's because I have a secret affinity for Zeus. It's because Catholic was the name of my first dog, who'd escape his leash to nip at the thighs of people of strictly Slovenian descent. I hope this dissimulative practice, some fifty years later, will spark an extremely niche bar fight. Until then, I'm content to point out that the name change indicated a change of heart upon the realization that the Holy Faith is the thing that remains, ever ancient and ever new—and certainly the thing I want to write about.

This book is an outgrowth of my blog, with a few of the

better essays from the *BadCatholic* thrown in, all united by the idea that, underneath the increasingly warm, stale discourses of politics and culture, there is God, the only freshness that does not grow warm. They aren't meant to be read in any particular order, only with a particular openness to criticism and the hope for an encounter with the one who surpasses all criticism and offers humanity, and even bloggers, perfect peace.

CULTURE

The Difference Between a Naming and a Baptism

I first cared about being Catholic not out of any profound love for the person of Christ but out of a profound distaste for my other options. That Jesus came, died, rose, and established a Church under the authority of the apostles united under Peter I take as a fact. I'm still learning to be attracted to it. That I'd sooner cut my own toes off than live life as, say, a self-proclaimed freethinker of the Reddit school—that was an immediate judgment of taste akin to not wearing Crocs.

My Catholicism only bubbled up from the realm of sensibility to one of genuine commitment during high school, where, among other misadventures, I was asked to use CE and BCE as the approved initialism with which to divide history instead of BC and AD. The switch was explained as a secularization of "Before Christ" and "Anno Domini" (in the Year of Our Lord) to CE and BCE, a switch that enabled us to refer to periods of history in continuity with the historians of the past without bringing in any "religious stuff."

The problem with this secularization is that it is not secular enough. CE and BCE refer to the "common era" and "before the common era," but this is a mere change of name. Within this framework, the entirety of history is still divided in accordance with the birth of Christ. Anyone with the vaguest spark of curiosity, upon learning time itself has been split like a watermelon, can still ask: What inaugurated this common era, this *Era Vulgaris*—the age of all peoples? What is the reason for the division? The secularist has not secularized history, he has merely obfuscated a Christianization of history, maintaining the fact and changing the name. Far from diminishing the Christian tradition, this obfuscation highlights it, as a veil may highlight a face, or as the obscurity of a stranger makes him all the more intriguing. To assume the importance of Christ, to know we live in this or that Year of our Lord while the ancients lived Before Christ—

> I LEARNED OF THE IMPORTANCE OF CHRIST THROUGH THE WEIRD AND FEARFUL FIRE REFLECTED IN THE EYE OF THE SECULARIST TRYING TO AVOID HIM.

this familiarity could breed contempt. But to discover the secret of history, to uncover, out of the vague and seemingly arbitrary BCE/CE rift, the astronomic importance of a strange and brilliant rabbi who healed the sick and claimed filial relation to the Almighty God—this puts an innocent, unassuming student into right relation with the Christ.

So it's not quite accurate to say it was a distaste for my

other options over a love for the person of Christ that drove me to the point of the Church. Rather, the other options are so hopelessly Christian they unintentionally accentuate the very person they try to downplay. I learned of the importance of Christ through the weird and fearful fire reflected in the eye of the secularist trying to avoid him. AD/BC showed the birth of Christ was important; CE/BCE shows it is indispensable. AD/BC was a practical bit of Christian reasoning; CE/BCE is a terrified inability to be anything but Christian. A website with the rather grandiose name of *Religious Tolerance* argued that, but can the religions of the world embrace a division of history based entirely on the birth of Christ now that Christ isn't in the name? What a subversive expansion of the Christian empire if they do!

The difference between Christianity and secularity is not the difference between two competing worldviews, faiths, or philosophies, but a difference between a meaningful universe and universal meaninglessness. The project of secularism has not been to assert anything nonreligious (how could one assert a "non"?), but to rename the religious. As BC/AD, the cathedral becomes the museum, Christmas becomes Wintertide, charity becomes philanthropy, the ethics of Christ become the ethics of rational human beings (with minor modifications), the sacrament of marriage becomes a ceremony, the City of St. Francis becomes San Francisco, baptism becomes a useful literary symbol, we forget the "holy" in "holiday," the "God be by you" in "goodbye," as the French forget the "*a dieu*" (to God) in adieu, the "sacre" in "*sacre bleu*," and the "tabernacle" in a French curse word. This renaming is really no more than a separation of things from their origins and of words from their meanings. The universe that results is obscure, awkward, ill-fit, absurd—everything without explanation. But this is the perverse blessing of secularism: The degree to which everything is without explanation is the degree to which Christianity asserts herself as the explanation.

Of course, the Church has appropriated pagan holidays, rituals, and objects. The objection really ought to be raised: "Might one not say the same thing of the Christmas tree, that it is a Christian renaming that hides an original meaning, one that will be uncovered, and is indeed being uncovered by the New Pagans of our generation?"

But the Church does not rename pagan traditions as the secularist renames Christian holidays, seasons, and symbols. The Church baptizes the world. A baptism gives a name, but the name is a consequence, symbol, and icon of something far greater—a change in the very being of the person baptized, who becomes, through baptism, a new creation, a child of God, and a member of the Church. A naming ceremony is a gentle thing, but a baptism is a violence and a death. In the former, a person is indicated as this person or that, taking on a new sign which will refer to him. In the latter, the person *becomes* this instead of that—the old is dead, the new has risen, and the name refers to this ontological change. In baptism, the person is christened, that is, made Christian. In a renaming, the person is made into nothing new—he is simply given a new referent.

The Church impudently gives pagan traditions new meanings, of which a new name is an icon and a consequence. The Winter Solstice is not renamed *Christmas* in the manner in which secularists timidly rename Christmas "Winter Solstice."

No, the Winter Solstice becomes Christmas—the old gods are dead and Christianity has killed them.

I believe this on the assumption, presupposition, and fantastic prejudice that Christianity is true, that her baptisms have the power to change the *raison d'etre* of things, for the simple reason that she speaks with the voice of the Creator from whom all meanings flow—actually, I believe all manner of absurdities. But even if we drop the Christian prejudice, it still remains true that, by virtue of the fact Christians really do believe they are changing the meanings of things, Christianity is doing something fundamentally different than the nonsensical renaming of Christian meaning by a post-Christian intelligentsia. If secularism renamed as the Church renames—staking a cross through this or that tradition and giving it a new

A NAMING CEREMONY IS A GENTLE THING, BUT A BAPTISM IS A VIOLENCE AND A DEATH.

meaning—then I could respect the Winter Solstice as something positive, something asserted over and against Christianity, something brave and, in the final account, human.

But our post-Christian renamings haven't the substance to offend. They are pious timidities before the specter of Christianity. They do not assert, as the Church asserted of Pagan traditions, the old gods are dead, demons, or the shadows and preparations of the one true God who has come into the world. They do not recreate, arguing that this tree, this season, this symbol, that all of this has a new meaning as, say, an Infinite

Universe Tree, the season of Self-Determined Meaning, the Feast of the Proclamation of the Dogma of Religious Pluralism. No secularist boldly declares the crucifix was always awaiting its fulfillment as the symbol of the Primacy of the Positive Sciences Over All Forms of Knowledge. The post-Christian cannot christen—he has not the potency. Secularism renames by watering down the strong, making broth out of the meat of Christianity. The secularist—may God bless him—can only pick some effect of the Christian meaning and claim this is all the Christian event *really* means: Christmas is really just a season of generosity, Easter really only a time of fertility, and so on. The problem is this: Watering down something to its effects lessens even the effects. Without the Christ Child, the spirit of generosity, family, or whatever one takes as the real, desacralized meaning of Christmas, far from glowing in

> IF I AM THE SAME THING AS MY FRIEND, COLLAPSED INTO HIM, IDENTIFIED-WITH, THEN MY LOVE FOR HIM IS NO GREAT LOVE. IT IS ONLY A LOVE OF SELF.

hearts, is extinguished by commercial advertising. Renaming Christmas as "a time for togetherness," a togetherness that only existed as an effect of a belief in that universal fraternity inaugurated by God becoming man, this destroys the cause and expects the effect. Is it really a surprise that, without its root, togetherness devolves into the grotesque pageantry of family feuding that is the parody of the Holy Day? The post-Christian renaming reduces to an acceptable effect without daring to alter the cause. The baptism invokes and declares a new cause—not spring, but Christ, not the gods, but God, not the garden's growth, but the Gardener. A cause alone can remain and bear the fruit of effects. An effect divorced from its cause—a holiday apart from a Holy Day—these crumble as a tree without roots.

If all of this is true, it would follow that the role of the Catholic in the post-Christian age is rather simple. He is to be a missionary of applied anamnesis, working with and loving his neighbors, not simply to radiate the ever-new love of Christ, but to midwife forth from them a recollection—a memory of God, one that reveals the world as one already contoured by his presence among us.

BEING FOR

Pope Francis is detested and loved for the same reason. Detested because his openness to the world seems to open the Church to sin by watering down Catholic identity into vague platitudes and passively accepting a corrupt culture while making leeway for vice. Loved, because this same openness seems to make mercy, redemption, and communion possible to so many who saw the Church as something closed.

In his High Priestly prayer, Christ prays for a specific group of followers he distinguishes from "the world." He goes so far as to say, "I do not pray for the world" (John 17:9). These words, taken on their own, could form the foundation of several brands of Calvinism and most of American Christianity. Jesus has a club where they can be with him for eternity. The rest, "the world," well, to Hell with them.

This attitude would be enough to damn Francis' "worldliness." But Jesus does not pray for the static salvation of his favorite people, nor does he cry out to the Lord of Heaven and Earth for isolated dollops of love onto a limited number of predestined foreheads. He prays for the unity of his chosen ones so *that the world may believe.* The world, distinguished from Jesus' "friends," is not distinguished from the Church by a distinction of the bad and the good, the damned and the elect. Rather, the distinction Christ makes is between those who believe and a world Christ *desires* to believe. We, the Church, are saved and unified in Christ, not to be pretty and sparkly and static, but for the salvation of the world.

Salvation, like everything Christ does, is not a finish line, but a new beginning, the ordination of a particular man into a being for others, the breaking-open and turning-out of the soul to the world. If God has called me to the Christian life, it is *not* because he is flexing his arbitrary power to save "whomsoever he will," all glory to him for saving me and not my neighbor. He chooses me *for* my neighbor. To be saved is to be *for*. The answer to the question why *I,* and not another, am Catholic is already written into the meaning of Catholic: universal. The universal donor can give to *all* blood types, the universal antidote counteracts *all* poisons, and the universal human being, the Catholic human being, must be all things to all people—a being for every other being, a being in a relationship of love to everything not Catholic.

What the what? The Catholic is fundamentally committed to loving the non-Catholic? It's tempting for the committed Christian to declare a violent, desert father-esque distinction between the Church and the world, to wash his hands, hide the kids, and walk backward from the dubious delights of modernity with middle fingers raised. We fear a radical catholicity and a universal availability that demands we enter into a relation of love with the world because we don't want to be tainted by its idiotic seductions. Surely this idea that the

Church is a solvent that can ingest any music, culture, activity, or custom, this "open Church," surely *this* is the cause of the crisis whereby the Church loses her identity and becomes indistinguishable from the world. Enough then, of this "loving the world" talk!

But this view, which understandably characterizes the horror many Catholics feel in our poverty-despising, baby-killing age, is more than grumpiness. It's bad metaphysics. Love, broadly and warmly described as being-for-another, is not a mingling of one with the other. It is not a total, or even a partial, identifying of one with the other, so that a loving husband strives to lose his sense of self by collapsing it into his wife's, or a friendship succeeds by virtue of a gradual annulment of difference between two friends into a gelatinous blob. The oneness established by love is only possible on the condition of a real distinction between the two participants in a loving relationship. If I am the same thing as my friend, collapsed into him, identified with him, then my love for him is no great love. It is only a love of self.

THE ONENESS ESTABLISHED BY LOVE IS ONLY POSSIBLE ON THE CONDITION OF A REAL DISTINCTION BETWEEN THE TWO PARTICIPANTS IN A LOVING RELATIONSHIP.

To love the world is not to mingle, identify with, or take on the life of the world, but to desire the good of the entire world as a constitutive motion of my very being. There is a division between the Church and the world only because a division is the necessary condition for the Church to love the world, to desire and work for its salvation according to the method Christ has established, namely, to establish a Church, his body, through which the world is saved. Christ divides only to draw all things unto himself.

Pope Francis confuses us because he seems to live this out, simultaneously distinct from and for the world, offering forgiveness for abortions without declaring abortion OK, distinguishing Church teaching from the world's doctrines of human sexuality while remaining fundamentally *for* the persons obeying these same doctrines. His catholicity offends, but I like it. It seems to me that salvation without the catholicity of the saved is an offense to human reason and an insult to the goodness of

WHAT CAN I DO IN ORDER THAT OTHERS MAY BE SAVED AND THAT FOR THEM, TOO, THE STAR OF HOPE MAY RISE?

God. For if the salvation of a single soul does not, by the same act, render that soul as a being for others, then to seek and attain salvation is a kind of ultimate selfishness—a man "pass[ing] through the battlefields with a rose in his hand," as Jean Giono puts it. God's gift of salvation, by this view, would always be at the exclusion of others, my acceptance always an assent to their exclusion. But Christ's method is the method of Love—we are saved *for* others. To preach salvation is not to expand the Saved Club. To preach salvation is to plead with the world to *join* us in the work of the Cross, to be saved for others, to be with us in a common labor of love that Christ has chosen as his method of wrenching a fallen world back to a Father of Lights. Catholicism is a task, not a state, and it is through this idea that we can best understand Francis' repeated demands to "get messy," to bring the Church to the outskirts of human existence.

As Pope Benedict says: "Our hope is always essentially hope for others; only then is it truly hope for me too. As Christians we should never limit ourselves to asking, 'How can I save myself?' We should also ask: 'What can I do in order that others may be saved and that for them, too, the star of hope may rise? Then I will have done my utmost for my own personal salvation as well.'" This gives new light and even self-evidence to that difficult teaching that there is no salvation outside of the Catholic Church: No one is saved apart from becoming Catholic—becoming universal, for all, desiring the salvation, not merely of self, but of neighbor, world, cosmos. Any claim to salvation outside of becoming Catholic (that is, any claim toward a salvation that stops at me and only extends to other people by another, extrinsic, unrelated act of God) is a false claim, a pretension to attaining Heaven as an individual, an isolated stamp on the forehead, a rubbing against everything the Bible teaches when it roots our personal salvation in our being-for and our damnation in remaining-for ourselves: "We know that we have passed from death to life because we love our brothers. Whoever does not love remains in death" (1 John 3:14).

We are Catholics in the age of the Two Popes. And what Popes! Francis lives out in the body and in terrifying, off-the-cuff declarations what Benedict suffered and struggled and succeeded to articulate in one of the most bitter, anti-Catholic periods of intellectual history. And what Benedict articulated is precisely this: the Catholic is best described by the word *for*. Francis, a son of the Church, is trying to show us what "for" looks like. Could we ask for more? Now is the Glorious and Triumphant Age of the Catholic Church, the moment for us, through the double encouragement of our living Shepherds, to become what we are by virtue of our baptism, in accordance with Christ's prayer that "the whole world may believe," to be for others, for the salvation of all, poor, detested, happy.

CHRISTIANITY AND THE CLAIMS OF EUROCENTRISM

I was recently called Eurocentric, in that I am A-OK with Christians hopping over to non-Christian countries and preaching the Very Good News of Jesus Christ. While I concede that preaching Christianity *could* be Eurocentric, and that many instances of said preaching *is* Eurocentric, the diehard association of the missionary Christian with the racist, swaggering white man is moronic.

First, it is no longer true that Europe is the center of world Christianity—that prize could equally go to the Americas or to Sub-Saharan Africa. If we *must* intrinsically link faith to a culture, then demographically speaking, it would be more accurate to call the pale, sunburnt missionary *Afro*centric.

Of course, we might say: "But African and South American faith *came* from Europe, from conquistadors, Jesuits, and the white people in *Things Fall Apart*, so still, this Christian mission stuff stinks of the rude imposition of European culture." That is: Christianity is not derived demographically, but historically, and historically speaking, Christianity came from Europe.

But if the first argument is unrealistic in the present

age, this one is racist in every age. To say that Christianity is Eurocentric has the unfortunate consequence of arguing that all non-European Christians are only Christians insofar as they bow to Europe. To assert that the preaching of one is domineering implies that the conversion of the other is submissive—and even sniveling. This, and not Christian missionary work, is Eurocentrism—the idea that Europeans may believe a certain creed, but non-Europeans can only be tricked into "belief" by powerful Europeans. This, and not preaching Christ, is racist—the vague notion that African Christianity is *actually* European. We feel mighty modern criticizing the Catholic missions to Brazil as inculturation. Do we not realize the insult we make in the same breath to the Brazilian? We have called him a powerless product of cultural force when he, on the level of religious experience, of prayer, creed, and personal identity, is calling himself a Catholic.

Statements of truth and falsity transcend culture. Whether there is a God, whether he is one or many, whether he communicates with his Creation; these are not culturally conditioned beliefs, but propositions that demand one's yay or nay. All of culture is put into question by the question of truth. To divorce the non-European from this experience is to divorce him from his humanity. To call his acceptance of Christianity an acceptance of Europe and its values (and never a rational, heartfelt decision of assent to the truth of a proposition) is to declare him unfit for the harsh climate of truth and falsity. But if the non-European is a human being, then he need not give a damn whether the proposition "God exists" comes from the palest of Presbyterians or the nearby palm tree—he may consider it and decide. The vision that seems to respect humanity by leaving it alone, fixated in custom and culture, is a horrible stunting of man's capacity. *Real respect for another culture is the assumption it can handle a truth that exceeds it.*

If it is argued that the Christian mission offers nothing true and thus does not and cannot transcend culture, then I say—hallelujah. Here is a criticism that has the piety to take Christianity as she offers herself. If Christianity is wrong, it is because she is utterly wrong, not because she comes from Spain. To make the move from the claim of Eurocentrism to the claim of falsehood is to begin to tackle the missionaries on the terms in which they mission—as bearers of the proposition: "God became man."

IF IT IS ARGUED THAT THE CHRISTIAN MISSION OFFERS NOTHING TRUE, AND THEREFORE DOES NOT AND CANNOT TRANSCEND CULTURE, THEN I SAY—HALLELUJAH.

Even if there was nothing racist about denying the non-European the ability to rationally and authentically believe a creed apart from inculturation, it remains true that Jesus was a Jew, and his apostles were Middle Easterners. Europe did not give birth to Christianity. She nurses what she received from Syria and Iraq. Calling this cry from the desert, this Jewish event, this Middle Eastern phenomenon, calling this Christianity European for the simple reason that Rome was bedazzled and converted by the poetry and strength of Bethlehem, Nazareth, and Jerusalem—

this seems Eurocentric. No one characterizes the Europeans who received Christianity from the Middle Eastern apostles as being "inculturated." Such a thing would be unthinkable. Christianity is the pushy power of white people—God forbid it be the triumph of the Jews. But it is true. Christianity began in Aramaic. The claim that Christian mission is Eurocentric is a subversive racism, in that conversion is only ever a submission to inculturation when Africans and South Americans are doing it—when Europeans convert to a proposition from the Middle East no one bats an eye. Europeans, apparently, have a natural superiority. They may convert and believe their brothers and sisters on other continents can only be mowed down by previous believers.

> WITHOUT GOD AND THE VALUES OF RELIGION, WE LOOK TO CULTURE TO FULFILL THE RELIGIOUS ASPIRATIONS OF MAN. CULTURE SURROGATES GOD.

It's true that Christianity has been spread as horrifically as Communism and as aggressively as global capitalism. Some evangelization really is Eurocentric. Some "mission work" is nothing more than tribal warfare writ large. But this is a temptation and a corruption of the Catholic, Christian faith, which involves a universal creed, a God relationship all men are capable of, and no tie to one nation or culture over another. The national Church is an idol. Those who conflate spreading Christ with spreading Coca-Cola are fools and antichrists. And Christians have been idolatrous fools, worshiping the nation in the guise of their God, calling conquest "mission" and nationalism "church." This impulse does not rise out of Christianity—it claws against it. Before the religionless go into raptures over their own innocuous uninvolvement with universal messages that purport to transcend culture, they should consider how the secular order is prey to precisely the same idolatry, worshiping a culture and a nation in the guise of some universal truth claim, national wars in the guise of democracy, extraordinarily Western notions of children, family, and sex in the guise of "women's rights," human experiments on foreign nationalities in the name of "science," and so forth. The sooner we get to the question of truth, shedding the ultimately indecisive shell of the world historical, the sooner we really deal with the problem of Christianity, and more importantly, the problem of the person, who, like a breathing truth claim, always transcends culture.

A final point can be made here. If it is true that the question of God transcends the importance of culture, then belief in God demands a radical generosity from every believing culture. Culture can no longer be an end unto itself—it must split open and give itself away in service to a higher value.

Catholics and Cultural Appropriation

There is no worse "cultural appropriator" than the Catholic. She prays on rosary beads (Italian appropriations of the Eastern European *chotki*, which is, arguably, a North African appropriation of the Hindu prayer rope). She regularly participates in Filipino devotions—without paying a modicum of lip service to being an imperialist pig. She worships before Mexican icons—which include symbolism rudely appropriated from the Aztecs. She hangs out with monks who appropriate the Jewish yarmulke by shaving the center of their heads (do they even care about the culturally embedded significance of the symbol?) and mimics innumerable pagan traditions around her Christmas tree.

She is shameless in indulging the fruits of culture because her Church posits a value *above* culture, a value in the light of which every culture abdicates its dubious position as the ultimate expression of humanity and becomes, instead, a servant. This value is the divine.

Consider a privileged, wealthy white man who enters a

black Baptist church in a low-income neighborhood and joins in singing a hymn. One interpretation—and surely this would be Tumblr's verdict—is that the man could not possibly understand the pain and suffering of the African experience of America, and by appropriating the fruits of this culture he commits a grave offense. Another—and this would be the naïve, religious interpretation of the same event—is that the true value of the hymn is not as an end but as a means. The hymn is for all humanity because the object of the hymn—Jesus—is for all humanity. Culture has become a vehicle toward something beyond any particular culture. Culture has become culture-for.

> **WHAT ONCE BELONGED TO THE PEOPLE AND THE NATION BECOMES FOOD FOR THE JOURNEY, HELP FOR ALL, AND MEANS FOR ATTAINING THE UNIVERSAL END OF EVERY INHABITANT OF EVERY NATION— FRIENDSHIP WITH GOD.**

What once belonged to the people and the nation becomes food for the journey, help for all, and means for attaining the universal end of every inhabitant of every nation— friendship with God. Culture-for-God gives itself away, abandoning itself to a humanity united by a common origin and destiny toward the divine.

Whenever we "try out" another culture because we think it groovy or indulge the illusion that the culture of the other is the "real" thing while our own, saturated with familiarity, is a pantomime, we commit the offense of dilettantism. We indulge acts without objects and profound motions without profound intentions. It is in this sense that the critics of cultural appropriation are correct to shoot their online frown out to the hipsters donning sacred headdresses at Coachella. But resentment over cross-cultural use in genuinely religious acts is an attitude that values the purity of race over the universal salvation of humanity.

The Catholic especially, whose very name means *universal,* either rejects this idolatry or rejects her or his catholicity. It is no accident that, from Día de los Muertos in Mexico to the crucifix of Chief Sitting Bull, the Church remains an icon of cultural appropriation. Mother of the Nations to those who love her, she is a tyrant and seductress of the noble savages to those who hate her influence—her audacious, transforming embrace of everything she deems good in the cultures she evangelizes.

It's in her nature. The Church is catholic precisely to the degree that, within her walls, all cultures abdicate their thrones and join in the service of the One God. Jealousy over cultural treasures in the Church (you cannot bless your house with chalk, you're incapable of sharing the historical meta-narrative of holy Poland!) is no sign of zeal, but of doubt in divine sovereignty. When culture becomes sacred, God becomes a household god. The decline of the Catholic Church, then, is not characterized by a growth in rational unbelief, but by a return to the local god, in which every culture is justified in and isolated to its own beliefs, values, and traditions.

Do we not see precisely this in the liberal panic over cultural appropriation? Without God and the values of religion, we look to culture to fulfill the religious aspirations of people. Culture surrogates God. It cannot be touched by those uninitiated in its mysteries nor imitated by those unconnected with its cult. White girls should not have cornrows, nor should anyone call anything "tribal" who is not in a "tribe." It is ineffable. It cannot be known outside of those who have experienced it firsthand, nor criticized by those who merely look in on it. Culture is divine.

On the other hand, "culture" is extraneous, a thing to be shuffled off as soon as it interferes with the "real," cultureless individual who exists under the trappings of culture. We laud those who escape the "traditional beliefs and values" of their "culture"—usually Jewish or Christian—and land safely on the side of Western values of free choice and individualism. Culture is the ultimate good, until your culture says abortion is bad, and then culture is bad. We work up a righteous sweat over scarves that look like the hijab while we approve of a foreign policy that introduces the Western logic of contraception to Muslim communities that oppose it. We promote the purity of the world's cultures while understanding they would all be better as democracies. Culture, in short, is sacred, but only insofar as it conforms to the basic doctrines of our post-Christian, Western culture. It is difficult not to see in this schizophrenia the aping of a lost belief: the sovereignty of God over all culture.

In the light of God's absolute transcendence, we have a real capacity for cultural criticism. We can say, with confidence, that it does not matter how historically important human sacrifice was to the Incas, there is a higher law than the law of culture, a law that judges human law and finds the Incas wanting. Cultural values do not justify themselves. Religion, in this respect, is *liberation* from tradition and freedom from the cult of ancestry, wherein evil is tolerated "as always having been" and ignorance persists under the guise of "custom." With God as its goal, no traditional behavior can be justified in itself, but only the degree to which it helps or hinders the attainment of holiness.

Now that God is dead, we ape this view as the phantom limb apes the limb. The West and its values play the part of the divine. An ambiguous slop of benefits and horrors spills from our beneficent, capitalistic, and "charitable" evangelization of the nations to the dubious gospel of post-Christianity. The nations are free to enjoy spicy food over Wonder Bread, but if the laws of culture defy the laws of Western liberalism, their claims to inviolability are rendered null. Instead of God, we have a Master culture, a set of historically embedded values and recent beliefs we earnestly take as absolute

AND A GOD WE WILL HAVE, WHETHER WE WANT ONE OR NOT.

norms of human behavior—and to which every knee shall bow. Post-Christian Western liberalism, with its basic doctrines of individualism, materialism, and secularism, demands servant status of the cultures it contacts without the common decency to declare itself a god.

And a god we will have, whether we want one or not— an absolute value to which all other values are subordinate. The only question is who we will end up worshiping. In this age, genuine acts of religion are always acts of defiance; they supplant the paltry god of current culture and assert that God alone is Holy, God alone is the value by which all others are ordered and judged.

Make Hell Hot Again

I have a problem with Hell that goes beyond squeamishness. The genuine possibility of an eternal separation from God doesn't bother me. If I am not free to reject Him, then human freedom is a sham, and the offer of an eternal marriage of the soul to its Maker is more akin to a rape. The logical possibility doesn't bother for the same reasons: Hell is compatible with an infinitely good God because it is not God but man who "creates" Hell by separating himself from his highest good. Rather, the problem is inserting the damned into God's end game—Creation brought to its triumphant completion. Doesn't the presence of everlasting torment put a damper on the success story?

I went to Aquinas for comfort only to find this problem accentuated. Aquinas describes sin as a disturbance of the Divine order, and that "so long as the disturbance of the order remains, the debt of punishment must remain also." Hell lasts forever because the disturbance of sin lasts forever. Aquinas makes this explicit when he argues that God "is forever unappeased by the punishment of the wicked." From this we must conclude the cosmic finale, the perfected universe in which all things are made new, could very well be described as the eternally disturbed order of an eternally unappeased God. However slight the imperfection, imperfection exists. Beyond our feelings of pity for this or that tormented soul, there still lingers the question of whether God is really so victorious if, at the end of the day, his order must endure this perpetual disturbance.

Paul MacDonald, in an essay for the *American Catholic Philosophical Quarterly*, mentions a classic argument in which "a world populated in the end by saints and sinners is a better cosmic whole than a world that contains only saints, because in the former world, where God brings at least some human beings to glory, and eternally as well as justly punishes the rest, God is

HELL LASTS FOREVER BECAUSE THE DISTURBANCE OF SIN LASTS FOREVER.

able to manifest his goodness the most clearly and fully." To me, this misses the point. The damned are a "disturbance of the divine order meriting punishment." What harmony can there be between order and a disturbance of that order? How can the problem of Hell be resolved by its place in the "cosmic whole" if Hell is a disturbance of that cosmic whole? Do we not, rather, have an infinite, agonizing tension of willed evil and divine punishment that triumphs over evil but does not eliminate it?

Throughout this inner debate, a decidedly unphilosophical voice kept making itself heard. My family would slip a prayer between the mysteries of the Rosary: "Save us from the fires of Hell, lead all souls into Heaven, especially those in most need of thy mercy." As the prayer kept repeating, something obvious entered my troubled mind: We pray that no one will go to Hell. The Catholic Church actively petitions for the salvation of all humanity. The Catholic must hold, under the threat of anathema, that God desires all to be saved, that he creates no being whom he wishes to be damned. While this saving action is the initiative of God alone, he undertakes this saving action in and through his Church, his body of believers on Earth. Saint Paul argues as much when he says that by his sufferings he is "filling up what is lacking in the afflictions of Christ" (Colossians 1:24).

If these premises are true, then the question of Hell always involves the questioner existentially, not simply because it is his eternal destiny that is discussed, but also because these premises make him coresponsible for the eternal destiny of others. A person's prayers, fastings, and sufferings are effective participations in the cross of Christ. They are the manner in which God has chosen to enact his desire to save all of humanity. One may take this "effective participation" in terms of merit and intercession, as when one prays that a person will not go to Hell, but one may also take this in a more mundane manner. If I get up from writing this article, cross the hall, and begin speaking with a colleague about Jesus, this action may help him reach Heaven. Through that conversation and others, he may develop the courage required to love God rather than reject him. I am, through the practice of charity, "doing the work of Christ," that is, participating in the salvific plan of God. The question of whether or not souls will suffer eternal torment rebounds upon the questioner, whose free actions join in the divine plan to save all souls from eternal torment. The argument can be summed up as follows:

Q: How can a just God allow souls to suffer Hell?
A: I don't know, how can you?

It is no accident that all supposed "answers" to the problem of Hell are also cogent arguments for a lack of effective participation in the salvific work of Christ to save all souls from Hell. If we say that Hell is not a genuine possibility, that it is not logically possible for a good God to permit it, then we have no need to pray "save us from the fires of Hell…lead all souls into Heaven." Such a prayer would be foolish and vain. If Hell is a logical impossibility of a good God, then, assuming God is good, we have no reason to ask for salvation. On the other hand, if we resolve the problem of Hell into a finally perfected Cosmos, we likewise get rid of the necessity to pray for the salvation of all the world. We may be motivated out of a personal sense of pity, but by this understanding, the eternal punishment of unrepentant souls is a fundamentally tolerable state of affairs.

Aquinas argues the damned will be useful, providing joy to the blessed and a warning to the living. MacDonald argues the damned could be described as benefiting the cosmic whole, allowing for the equal display of God's justice as much as God's mercy. To ask the question somewhat rudely: Why should we pray against such a fate? If eternal torment is something useful, reflective of God's goodness and freely chosen by the sinner, what motivation do we have to pray for the salvation of those who freely choose? The answer cannot be "pity" or "sympathy" because, according to Aquinas at least, these are precisely the kind of emotions we will not feel. Aquinas argues we will rejoice in the justice of God displayed in the cries of the damned. And in the end, any description of a perfected Cosmos including the damned as "harmonious" implies we have no need to pray for the salvation of all out of a concern for a final cosmic scenario in which "every tear will be wiped away." By this view, cosmic perfection is just as attainable with or without souls in Hell. Where, then, does the urgency of the prayer of the Church for the salvation of all humanity come from?

IF HELL IS A LOGICAL IMPOSSIBILITY OF A GOOD GOD, THEN, ASSUMING GOD IS GOOD, WE HAVE NO REASON TO ASK FOR SALVATION.

It is in the interest of those beings coresponsible with Christ for the salvation of all humanity not to solve the problem of Hell on the level of speculation, precisely because they are called to solve the problem of Hell on the level of action, to act in such a way that no soul suffers Hell's eternal fires. We are made responsible for others through our participation in the cross of Christ when Hell remains problematic, when we cannot conceptualize a God-perfected universe that includes the screams of torment.

It is in the very tension between our inability to become intellectually satisfied with the presence of eternal suffering and the simultaneous affirmation that Hell must be a possibility of human freedom that we are given to ourselves as actors, cocreators, workers in the vineyard, missionaries—beings with something to do. Cosmic harmonies might work well for the Buddhists but send Christians to sleep. If God wills humanity to participate in his act of salvation, what better way to encourage their participation than by making Hell unthinkable, intolerable, and yet possible?

The kingdom rallies against the anti-kingdom precisely when the latter takes on the quality of the unthinkable-possible-evil. But this is too poetic: The kingdom rallies when you and I go about the world doing the work of God that saves people from everlasting death. And isn't this what the Church has always said?

Technology

Netflix and the Culture of Choice

I f freedom is an exploding horizon of possible options, I'll take some mild form of oppression. The eternal possibility of another option isn't a space to stretch my arms and sing the national anthem—it is the paralysis of the human person into grotesque inaction. This is exemplified by Netflix.

To sit down and choose any movie out of the massive expanse of options Netflix offers is nearly impossible. Every choice is plagued by the immediate availability and advertised possibility of a better choice lurking in the scroll-down. The law, I think, is this: The longer it takes a group of friends to choose a single movie from the options available to them, the less appealing each choice looks. Every apprehended option speaks of better unapprehended options. We become saturated with possibility. The prospect of actually choosing something becomes a point of anxiety.

The idea that freedom blossoms from a mere diversity of choice and the constancy of another option becomes supremely suspect ten minutes into movie-searching, as we begin to employ methods to protect ourselves from the abyss of choice—narrowing ourselves to five choices, employing a democratic voting system, setting ourselves a time limit, or forcing ourselves to remain in a genre. In short, we initiate processes of restriction and lawmaking. We begin our Netflix search as free-and-easy hipsters of the Choose-Whatever Generation—we end as fascists. And even with our self-restrictions, we usually end in frustration, saying, "Let's just do this one!" We confess, in the end, that *any* option is better than wallowing in the paralysis of possible options.

> WE BEGIN OUR NETFLIX SEARCH AS FREE-AND-EASY HIPSTERS OF THE CHOOSE-WHATEVER GENERATION—WE END AS FASCISTS.

But this paralysis is not cured by our eventual choice. Finally watching the movie is not characterized by relief. We do not rest in our choice. "If it's really bad," we say, "we can still choose another one." We watch our movie through the lens of another possibility that floats over our vision like a specter and makes the movie we watch the object of intense judgment. We are ready to abandon ship (at least until the movie sells itself to us).

It's not that bad—is it? After all, this is an unusual situation. Usually you approach Netflix with some idea of what you want to watch, and this frame restricts your choice and saves you from paralysis. True—and that's quite the point—but this isn't really about Netflix.

Our culture is plagued (which only ever means *I* am plagued and I believe it of others) with an aversion to the given—those people, places, and things that are given to us, annihilating the possibility of another person, another place, and another thing.

Marriage—legally and culturally speaking—is no longer a self-restriction of existence, by which I promise myself to another and thereby rip myself from the possibility of doing otherwise. The very possibility of divorce and prenuptial agreements keeps the door open to another possibility—a "better" way. Is it a surprise that my generation is moronic about the idea of marriage, and more than moronic, deathly frightened of ever choosing it, preferring the dialect of trying-it-out over till-death-do-us-part in our banal adventures in cohabitation? How difficult it is to choose an unfragmented, holistic life; how difficult it is to promise ourselves to something; how difficult it is to maintain that purity of heart that wills one thing (Kierkegaard) when the very air we breathe exalts the freedom of choice.

The myth is that we will be enabled to choose what we really want in this atmosphere. The reality is that we are terrified from choosing anything at all, and worse, that even in choosing we don't choose—we try. What do we call a marriage open to the possibility of divorce? If it works, did it really work? If I die un-divorced, did I stay faithful to my vows? Or did I try marriage out, right up to the point of death, a Netflix choice forever haunted by a possibly better option?

The awful is everywhere. It is in the way we work; we are expected to keep several jobs, to move often, to be ready to drop whatever it is we are doing at the whiff of a better option and a little more money. It is in the way we approach our bodies.

Gender is described as an open-ended possibility of virtually infinite choice, and we are encouraged at an early age to self-identify with a particular sexuality, gender, and orientation. Far and fading is the terrifying *given* of a body that must be reckoned with, creeping closer is the ocean of choice, the panic of which usually ends in a nondecision—a regular taking up of different sexualities, a lifelong toying with identity, or that paralysis by which we settle into the nondescriptiveness of being nothing at all. It is in the way we treat our communities—as inherently leavable for another option. It is in having children. Abortion allows us to try having kids instead of doing it.

The logic of the people who support abortion is not some bizarre misdirection. It is a proper blossoming of a capitalistic misconception of freedom that the virtue of freedom is not in making the right choice but in the possibility of choice itself—the supposed "power" of consumers and their promise of satisfaction. And so we are "pro-choice." The possibility of another option to pregnancy is a value in itself—even when that other option involves killing a child.

This, this is the millennial farce. We are tourists of our hometowns, dilettantes of our work, taste testers of our relationships, and brief visitors of the geography of our own bodies, all permanence and givenness haunted and negated by the siren song of somewhere, someone, something else. We indulge the same illusion that a Netflix party indulges—that more possibilities will make us happy, increasing our chances of making the right choice and ending up satisfied. But as with Netflix, choice as an open-ended category paralyzes us from ever really *doing* anything. And when we do lurch into action, the possibility of another option haunts our decisions and transforms them into tentative tests. We never really annihilate ourselves from the primordial soup of possibility.

The opposite of this mode of being is adventure, a mode I would roughly define as a knock on your door that makes you get off your ass to do something. Adventure is a synthesis of freedom and necessity—a free, creative dealing with what is *given*. It involves reckoning with what you do not choose. We would do well to make use of G.K. Chesterton's formula here, that an adventure is only an inconvenience rightly considered. An inconvenience is given as an annihilation of other possibilities. It is an inconvenience to be born into a particular family and a particular body; to have a home in a particular place, a vocation to this particular man or woman, or a project of work no one else can do.

WE NEVER REALLY ANNIHILATE OURSELVES FROM THE PRIMORDIAL SOUP OF POSSIBILITY.

An inconvenience rightly considered is not haunted by the possibility of another choice. It is a restriction. We cannot do otherwise. We promise not to do otherwise. We are made terribly responsible.

Adventure is a mode fundamentally opposed to the paralysis of our culture. Against the vagueness of being able to do anything at all, against the absurdity of placing value in the mere ability to choose something else, adventure is an acceptance of what is given in all its thorniness, tragedy, and splendor. To be on an adventure is to reduce, to limit, to burn the bridges that no one else can burn at the terrible expense of any "other choice" or "better place." In this is our profound, existential experience of freedom.

Freedom chooses its necessities. Paradoxically, we are most certain that we are free when we freely determine ourselves; when we take care of the land we belong to and destroy in ourselves the possibility of moving; when we make a vow and keep it; when we give ourselves a moral law and obey it; when we admit that we, without our choosing, have been given to a family and a community and give ourselves to them. Freedom is felt when we destroy "the other option."

A life made sharp by the vow, the promise, the firm decision and the whittling of that glut of possibility into the narrow point of actuality—I want it. I want to cease coddling an extended not-doing and nonchoosing, to stop indulging that constant potency which, for the mere fact of its ending in death, we call a life. Who is free, finally? The man who knows that no action of his ever annihilates the possibility to do otherwise, or the monk who vows poverty, chastity, and obedience?

The Gospel on Your iPad

Books are solid. This is at once a physical description and a metaphysical one, and it is on this metaphysical solidity that we ought to ground our loyalty to the book over and against the allure of the ever-changing screen.

A book is solid in the warm way a friend is solid: direct, dependable, honest, and reliable. It stands on its own. It is relinquished by the author once it is published. Now a solitary object, it exceeds his power. He can no longer edit, add to, or subtract from its content. It has a fate and a destiny of its own, a freedom to be read, interpreted, and used quite apart from the power of its author.

The online text, on the other hand, remains within the ministrations of controlling powers. Tomorrow it might be updated by its author, deleted by its web host, moved by the publisher, or reformatted by an intern with big ideas about Maximum Ad-space Efficiency. And who in the academic world has not had the experience of going to an online journal to revisit some article or other, only to find that the journal has updated its policies and now requires—$33.99! Who has not experienced the disappointment of a broken hyperlink? The screened text exists under the shadow of change.

It's not just the hosting websites and their fluctuating policies. All screened texts depend on electricity, design, and, in general, the functionality of the machine that enables its display. The book also needs creators to make it sturdy and readable. But once it is in my hands, no ongoing work of bookbinders or printers or wholesalers sustains its existence. The screened text alone requires constant sustaining work in the present moment of reading. I continue to read from a screen as long as a power company burns coal or harvests wind to supply me with energy. I can read the online text as long as Verizon or McDonald's free Wi-Fi supplies me with an internet connection. I do not "turn the page" of a Kindle. I click, and in clicking depend on the coding of experts and the manufacturing of more experts to work in a preordained fashion that

I CAN READ THE ONLINE TEXT AS LONG AS VERIZON OR MCDONALD'S FREE WI-FI SUPPLIES ME WITH AN INTERNET CONNECTION.

I do not understand—one that results in a "page turn." The present moment of my reading rests on continued coherence and compatibility between the coding of my device and the formatting of my text. We do not recognize this dependence until we are required to update our device or buy a new one. Here the seams in seamless uploading always seem to show. We become frustrated—shocked, even—to find our act of reading at the mercy of manufacturers.

In a very real sense the screened text is held out for viewing, available to us at any moment only because it is supported, as our occasional and sometimes desperate calls to tech support remind us. We may own books. The thought that we "own" an e-book or a PDF in the same way is an illusion. In reality, we possess an e-book or an online article only by virtue of the cooperation of the publisher, web-hosting service, electricity company, internet provider, manufacturer, and some kid writing the code to effect the data migrations that allow us to continue to view it on some yet-to-be-invented device that will undoubtedly (and soon) supersede what we now use.

When we think of metaphysically solid objects, worthy of predicates like "dependable" and "honest," we think of simple tools like the hammer and nail, meals like meat and potatoes, warm and wonderful objects with clear purposes: axes, mugs, candles, windows, boxes, doors, altars, fences. They are the stuff symbols are made of, for the symbol relies on the meaning of a thing immanent in its appearance. The book is like this. It was made to be read. It shines with its own evident purpose. It is as honest as the hammer. It is itself and its symbol: knowledge, learning, and reading are immanent in its very appearance, which is why a home with a well-stocked bookshelf conveys the impression of a well-stocked mind. This, as much as its freedom from controlling and sustaining powers, is a source of its metaphysical solidity.

A multipurpose object loses that quality of solidity possessed by a thing whose purpose is singular and direct. Smartphones, cars with myriad accessories, chairs with cup holders, adjustable headrests, and mechanical functions transforming it into a bed—these things have their place, but as their purpose is obscured in multiplicity, they do not resonate with the quality of solidity. They are "intruded upon" by too many functions. No one makes a symbol out of a 14-in-1 Home Entertainment System.

The screen is the ultimate multipurpose tool. It may be used for reading an essay—but it need not. I may equally watch some show on Netflix, play a Flash game, check my bank account, or perform math equations. Anything I am reading could, in the same mode, and on the same screen, become something else. This is the phenomenology of the screen: It could be otherwise.

Every student understands this, and rather painfully so. This or that essay made manifest on a screen could equally become Facebook, or cat videos. It is a common critique of computers that they distract us from our work. True, but the problem is not limited to the moments in which they distract us. The experience of reading a text that could be otherwise is fundamentally different from reading a text that couldn't. We may be distracted away from a book, but we are never distracted from the book by the book. The screen, by contrast, is by its very nature distracting. Everything it presents is precarious, haunted by the specter of alternatives. It is no more "just another way of reading" than speaking to a person who could at any moment be replaced by some other person is "just another way of speaking." It is a *different* way of reading.

This is the main reason we feel the book to be solid compared to the screen. The screen is saturated with possibilities. It is fluid.

When everything is presented as a momentary manifestation of what could be otherwise, information takes on a frightening quality of sameness—this murder, that funny BuzzFeed quiz, this revolution in the Middle East, that argument for atheism, this portrait, that meme. As each item replaces the last, our responses are slowly reduced in their complexity and emotional content, until finally we gaze with internet eyes: We either "like" or dislike. Everything is either interesting or uninteresting. We are stimulated or not stimulated. There are many causes of the homogenization of all knowledge into the sphere of interest, but the screen makes it eminently possible by presenting everything as possibly everything else.

This encourages a distinct mode of thinking. Our current skepticism is not a conclusion of any intellectual exercise. We have not taken up nonchalance, irony, triviality, and black humor as weapons against an absurd universe or a bankrupt intellectual system, as a Camus or a Kierkegaard might have. We have not thought through problems of knowledge, God, or existence and come to the grounded and reasoned conclusion that "life is what you make of it," or that "folks have their own truths." Ours is an emotional skepticism, a screenlike sensibility in which the world is something watery, a flux of possibilities without fixed points of truth, without anchors of belief.

> THE SCREEN...IS BY ITS VERY NATURE DISTRACTING. EVERYTHING IT PRESENTS IS PRECARIOUS, HAUNTED BY THE SPECTER OF ALTERNATIVES.

Is it any wonder that even the most self-evident truths take on the qualities of the screen through which they are presented?

A Wikipedia article on Einstein and an argument for God's existence posted on Reddit are altered in their significance, value, and effect on our lives, not by their content but by virtue of being presented as saturated and haunted with the presence of other-words and other-videos, possible-porn and possible-Facebook, held in front of us by mechanical and personal powers that might do otherwise than faithfully hold up the text. What good is it for us to present the most wonderful of truths if the very mode by which we present them is in flux? Moses may as well have carved the Ten Commandments in melting ice.

Public educators, all too aware of the apathy of the rising generation and the ineptitude of the modern high-schooler, wish to solve these problems by promoting the screen instead of the book. Online classes, video learning, computers for every student, greater internet access for the entire nation, Smart Boards, online forums—the optimism that believes a generation of children will be profoundly improved by an even deeper investment in the screen is wrongheaded. True, with the screen I can do what the most brilliant and erudite Renaissance man could only dream of: access translations of Plato, Aristotle, Augustine, and Aquinas and compare them and contrast them without cost or effort; learn about every animal and plant species categorized on this good earth; map the stars with a finger. If access to content were the only issue, we would be in the midst of a second Renaissance. But the form in which

IF YOU WANT TO DESTROY A CHILD'S LOVE FOR LEARNING, GET RID OF BOOKS.

content is given informs the content. The screen is in flux. It teaches us that nothing is solid and nothing can be trusted to endure.

If you want to destroy a child's love for learning, get rid of books. Serve him Plato from a PDF and E.B. White from an e-reader. Banish from his formative years any experience of objects that incarnate immaterial thought. Remove the impractical, antiquated book in all its stubborn solidity, and encourage the child to dive into the flux wherein everything could be otherwise. If we do this absolutely, if we ensure that not even the rumor of books reaches our rising generation, we will create a new man for the digital age: a puddle of disconnected thoughts pretending to have a head.

Though a concern for the stubborn maintenance of physicality is a concern for everyone, it is of special concern to the Catholic. Saint Thomas Aquinas argued that every real being is a unity of form and matter. The intelligible form of the thing (or the idea or the essence) is expressed in and through the physical stuff that makes it up—the matter. The human person, for instance, is a particular unity of body and soul—the soul is the form of the body. It animates the body and forms it in its particular qualities. This unity cannot be separated except in death. In death, the body loses the intelligible, animating, forming principle we call the soul, and thus it fades into an unintelligible, inanimate, formless corpse.

The book is an artifact that teaches us about this unity. The ideas of the author, the thoughts and visions of the poet—these are all expressed and manifested in and through the material of the printed page. This relation of the spiritual to the physical forms one solid object—the book—much in the same way that the relation of the soul to the body does not form a duality, but a unity—the human person.

Catholics are accustomed to seeing books not as a mere translation of ideas into the physical world but as unities of the spiritual and physical. Within the Catholic liturgy, at the end of the Gospel, the priest kisses the book in which it is contained. Often, the priest picks up the Gospels and blesses the people with them, moving the heavy book in a sign of the cross. These activities would make no sense if the physical stuff that manifested the inspired ideas of the Gospel writers were merely incidental conveyors of meaning. It is only because the physical object, the book, forms a unity with the words it manifests, that it can be approached, not just as a conveyor of meaning, but an object of reverence. We can kiss the Gospel, and thereby reverence the Good News of Jesus Christ, or because the physical Gospel and the words of Christ exist in physio-spiritual union in the object we call the book.

It would be silly to press this too far. The book, after all, is an artifact, not a natural being. If one separates the form and the matter of the human person, that person dies, but it would be excessive to argue that dropping your Missal in a puddle has such a drastic effect on the words of the Mass. Nevertheless, our books are objects of possible reverence and irreverence only because they, to some degree, really make present in a single object the word of God. This is why, despite the convenience they offer, Catholics should resist the tendency to turn prayer books into PDFs and missals into iPhone apps. If we would flinch to see a priest, upon finishing the Gospel reading, kiss the iPad upon which it was displayed, it is because we already have an inkling of the difference between a sacramental unity and a mere conveyor of content. The physical iPad does not exist for the Gospel. It does not form a unity with words of Matthew, Mark, Luke, and John, such that they are manifested by its very physical bulk. The screen could be otherwise. It may convey the Gospels for a moment; it may convey cat videos in the next. It never forms a unity with what it manifests; the physical iPad is not formed by the spiritual ideas of the Gospel writers. To kiss an iPad in an act of reverence to the Gospels misses this fact and misses what is unique about the Catholic experience, that in the Incarnation of Christ, in which God takes on flesh, the very physical stuff of this world is married to the spiritual, not in mere incidental expressions of the spiritual, but in real, unified objects and events, in signs and sacraments, in things and stuff, in people and places, God among us.

THE SCREEN COULD BE OTHERWISE. IT MAY CONVEY THE GOSPELS FOR A MOMENT; IT MAY CONVEY CAT VIDEOS IN THE NEXT.

Sex

CELIBACY IN THE LGBTQ AGE

I t doesn't matter, statistically speaking, that there is no correlation between the celibate life and sexual abuse. It doesn't matter that, as a 2004 study of the issue showed, children are one hundred times more likely to be sexually abused by a teacher than a priest. It doesn't matter that celibates tend to be pretty much as boring as everyone else. We are ideologically and culturally armed against the normalization of celibacy—spiritually committed to the image of the "dirty priest."

That is to say, we're Protestant. Long before our brilliant memes and the anticlerical cartoons of *The New York Times*, the Reformers were cranking out suspicion of this "no sex" stuff. Luther still reverberates in the cultural consciousness of even the hippest of sexologists: "That unhappy state of a single person, male or female, reveals to me each hour of the day so many horrors, that nothing sounds in my ear as bad as the name of monk, or nun, or priest." American anti-Catholicism was similarly haunted. Throughout the 1920s, the Ku Klux Klan made the word *celibacy* code for being a man-whore. They passed out titillating tracts such as "Why Priests Should Wed"

and "The Inevitable Crimes of Celibacy: The Vices of Convents and Monasteries, Priests and Nuns."

Our amateur reading of Freud (repression = bad) put the finishing pedophile-mustache onto our sketch of the cleric and hiked the habit of our imaginary, wanton nun. Even the word *virgin* has been transvalued into a pornographic ad word, meaning, from what I understand, desperate to be anything *but*.

In a certain respect, it's for the best. Better to have an unjustified stereotype as a motivation to clean out the Church than clerical pride that sweeps the problem under the rug. But even as we enjoy the pleasant, morally cleansing tradition of calling priests pedophiles, let's not delude ourselves. We do not view celibacy with suspicion because we have looked at the numbers and determined that priests and nuns have the greatest likelihood of abusing children or being sexually indecent. There already exists an American stereotype of "the dirty celibate," indulged as much in pornography as it is defamed in pop psychology, and we allow genuine cases of sexual abuse to reinforce this preexisting image.

On The One Hand, We State That Sex Is *Never* A Need.

But our blanket disdain for celibacy is beginning to look a little phobic in the LGBTQ+ age. Given our recently broadened understanding of human sexuality, can we sustain our criticism of celibacy?

On the one hand, we state that sex is *never* a need. It does not matter how a woman is dressed, nor how she dances, nor what she says—no man ever *needs* to have sex with her. He is always in control. He is always responsible for his actions. Sex is not an act one *has* to perform on the basis of external stimuli, no matter how tempting. The idea that "she was asking for it" is utterly reprehensible for this reason. How can we hold this view and simultaneously blame the sex-abuse scandals on celibacy, as if the lack of sex leads to abuse by logical consequence? Sex is never a need for the frat boy, but it is for the seminarian?

The criticism of celibacy on the basis of "male need" perpetuates a culture of rape, wherein any deprivation of the male from sex becomes an evil. This is the dark underside of the cry to "let priests marry!" As often as it means "let's reasonably consider the Eastern tradition of a married priesthood," it means "give these men some women before they do something terrible with their sex drive." Women become the necessary punching bag for the male libido—men become monsters. Consider how all of our flowery prose about love, promise, commitment, and form has been handily reduced to the ethical demand that anything "sexual" be performed between "consenting adults." This is American Sex at its finest. Our love of freedom provides the "consent." Our state government provides the definition of "adult." Between these two normative principles, our genital activities are justified. If we can avoid being a rapist on the one hand and a legal child molester on the other, we've got ourselves an ethical sex life, conducive to human flourishing, evident in the beaming joy with which we wake up and consider how wonderfully integrated we are with our sexuality.

But can we preach that "choice" is the fundamental determinant of the ethical sexual act while we cast a scornful and pitying glance on our priests and nuns, who *choose* never to have sex? It seems that choice is only a morally determining factor if you end up having sex. If you choose *never* to have sex, your choice is suspicious. The girl at the party who says, "no, I do not consent" practices her free will and demands respect as the very icon of sexual ethics. The girl at the same party who says, "no, I do not consent, nor will I ever" is a slave of the Roman Church, brainwashed and shamed into a cloister.

We can no longer pretend a sexuality that doesn't have sex is a fundamentally bad thing. Asexuality, for instance, is a positive *type* of sexuality, a sexual identity with a movement, a nonprofit agency, and a flag. One might argue that while the asexual does not choose to be asexual, the celibate chooses to be celibate. What is biologically and psychologically determined in the asexual is chosen for a spiritual reason by the celibate—even at the complaint of her "biology." As such, it is unnatural.

This critique shatters against LGBTQ+ ethics, which have long decried the idea that a sexual identity is only justified if it is biologically determined. The search for the "gay gene" is over. As Suzanna Walters wrote for *The Atlantic*, the view that one must be "born this way" in order to justify a sexual behavior is left over from our hetero "ideology of immutability" and a denial of the complexity of sexuality. Sexual identity is not determined from the beginning, but remains "fluid" and "complicated" throughout one's entire life. There is a "power in choosing to be gay," for it is "not our genes that matter here but rather our ethics," Walters writes.

By this logic, it is false to fault the celibate for choosing celibacy rather than following his or her "natural inclinations," and it props up the violent, hetero-normative idea that only what is grounded in biology can be "real."

We laud the nobility of the pansexual who doesn't see gender, who isn't attracted to the "visible sex" but to the soul and the *personality* of the desired person. We add to our exponentially growing list of possible identities the demisexual, which is, to quote their website, "a sexual orientation in which someone feels sexual attraction only to people with whom they have an emotional bond." Part of our developing ontological system is the validation of those desires that move beyond the body as definite forms of sexuality. Can we maintain this and still accuse the sister of sublimating her earthly desire

ASEXUALITY IS A POSITIVE TYPE OF SEXUALITY, WITH A MOVEMENT...AND A FLAG.

for sex into phony visions, or lambaste the priest, as author Michael P. Carroll does, for "spiritualizing" his carnal desires into a devotion to the Blessed Virgin Mary? It seems that it's good to be free of a narrow attraction to particular bodies, but only as long as one is still having sex. It is good to see past the physical form only insofar as one still gets to enjoy it. But if a man actually decides to devote the creative energy of human sexuality to spiritual realities, he's a freak.

There is a common theme in all this. Any sexual activity is good, natural, and healthy *except* choosing not to have sex.

Spiritualization is good as long as one still has sex. Asexuality is good as long as it's a natural feeling, and not a choice to abstain from sex. Choice is good, as long as it always leaves open the possibility of choosing sex. Philosopher Slavoj Žižek points this out as a symptom of our late-capitalist society, "enjoyment becomes a kind of a weird perverted duty":

> *This is the difference between the modern and the postmodern: when that other pornographic book was published,* Lady Chatterley's Lover, *it was banned at once. This is good, very healthy indeed. Pornography that is not banned at once, you know, it is like coffee without caffeine, beer without alcohol, a proletarian movement without the Absolute, and so on, and so on. But this book, the* Fifty Shades of Grey *book, it is embraced openly, the women read it on public transport, and so on, and so on. It is the Other without Otherness, utterly obscene. In the liberal society, everything is permitted, every kind of sexuality; not only permitted, it is mandatory. The command everywhere is this: you must Enjoy! The truly radical act, this I claim, is to not enjoy.*

What if, in an age of mandatory enjoyment, the celibate is the last radical?

All of this has an obvious root, though it seems mean-spirited to mention. Our sexual ethics shy away from sexuality considered as an *act* of the person and instead consider sexuality as an *identity*. In older theories of virtue, who I am is a result of what I do. If I perform acts of courage, I will build within myself the habit of courage, and will become a courageous person. Within our current sexual ethic, it is precisely the reverse: What I *do* is the result of *who I am*. An activity—having sex with person X—is justified through an ontology—being this type of person Y.

This identity saves me from my freedom. It fixes me into a type of person. I am no more responsible for the sexual preferences, value responses, and acts that flow with necessity from my sexual identity than I am responsible for the fact that "thinking linguistically" or "not being able to fly" flows from my identity as a human being.

If a past generation panicked over not educating their desires, passions, and activities in conformity with that mysterious, invisible, unchanging moral law that reason ascertains, I panic over finding my identity—that mysterious, invisible, unchanging core of my person that justifies my desires, passions, and activities. I still feel the burning *ought* of sexuality, the need to conform my sexual acts within some order—the only difference is that the normative order is in *me*. Sin is no longer "not doing as I ought" but "not being who I am." No one will sneer at me for indulging in a threesome, only for being "inauthentic," "closeted," or "repressed." *I must enjoy,* because who I am is the type of being (heterosexual, pansexual, omnisexual) who enjoys X—and I am obligated to "be myself."

The happy nun contradicts the deterministic ethics of sexual identity. Her life embodies the fact that our sexuality is not a determined lump of the drives we happen to feel at any given moment, nor a mystical identity we find one day, but the question of what we *do* with our drives as they present themselves. In the life of the celibate, sexuality is fully revealed as a project we are responsible for, rather than a fixed identity we mutely affirm and acknowledge (and later panic as our drives shift, our desires change, and our identity changes with it).

The celibate does not deny a sphere of sexuality nor belittle its beauty and importance. The celibate denies that this sphere exists outside of our freedom. The celibate does not deny orientations, feelings, and drives that present themselves as given and will not be rationalized away. The celibate denies that identity is found in these feelings and drives; instead believing our identity is shaped by *what we make of them.* In accepting a call to radical, frightening

> THE CELIBATE DOES NOT DENY A SPHERE OF SEXUALITY NOR BELITTLE ITS BEAUTY AND IMPORTANCE.

freedom, the celibate's primary question is how sexuality will be integrated into his or her *entire* person, rationality, spiritual destiny, value apprehension, conscience, lived body, and membership in the human community—that alone constitutes a true identity. This freedom is summed up by Joseph Cardinal Ratzinger's directive, given in the eighties and still as radical as the day it was written: "Today, the Church provides a badly needed context for the care of the human person when she refuses to consider the person as a 'heterosexual' or a 'homosexual' and insists that every person has a fundamental

Identity: the creature of God, and by grace, his child and heir to eternal life."

We want freedom—as long as it's a freedom we are not responsible for. We want a political freedom not to be oppressed in our sexual identity, but not the personal freedom to say no to a feeling, desire, or drive. As long as the celibate is a sign of contradiction in an age of calcified identity, we will wistfully imagine the nun as secretly diseased and the priest as typically abusive. The "crimes of the monasteries" must be inevitable because sexuality must be inevitable—lest we all become responsible.

An Aside on Lust

ust is love frightened of family. Lust is love frightened of its own creativity, frightened of being swept into the cocreation of a new world and the total life kisses contain as an objective possibility. Lust prefers to hold communion back to a safe number of controllable feelings and sensations. Lust runs scampering at the sight of offspring, vows, permanent living spaces, mutual labor, difficulties, titles, name changes—all those signs and symbols of love's power to make us *new*.

Anonymity is the soul of lust. Aquinas explains this in monkish fashion: If, in the sexual act, "it is not as a wife but as a woman that a man treats his wife" it is a sin. Lust is love scared to love the other as wife, as husband, as a relational reality that reflects back upon me and makes me into a new kind of being and a new kind of life. One can love a woman and be anyone at all. One can love his wife only in and through being her husband. One can love a man and remain unchanged. One can only love the father of her children in and through being a mother. The fear of love, which is lust, is a fear of ecstasy, a fear of being drawn out of ourselves and into what is new.

Lust never wants to meet the parents. Any evidence of

the other having a definite life, a childhood, a family (which contains, in erotic love, the possibility of becoming *your* family, changing you once more), is an offense against anonymity, of the other as a woman or a man or a real nice guy. This is scary because, as philosopher Martin Buber would put it, the I in relation to the Thou is a new kind of I. Ain't nobody wanna be a new kind of I. Ain't nobody. And so lust avoids those moments that make the anonymous other appear as a specific *you*.

Our absurd fear of pregnancy has its roots here. In pregnancy, we become a new kind of person—a parent. We want sexual love to free us, but the advent of the child reveals sexual love as a limiting force—one that whittles us down into husbands, wives, fathers, mothers, workers.

If freedom is the absence of limitation, love negates freedom. If freedom is more than an absence of limitation (a freedom from), if it reveals itself as an opportunity (a freedom for), then love crowns freedom. I, for one, am free in order to be limited. Love limits us, and life is a long learning to love being limited.

Life Cycles

Our painful attempts to live a fulfilling sexual existence could be helped by considering the world of agriculture. This idea is hardly novel, and it owes much to that fine essay by author and farmer Wendell Berry, "The Body and the Earth." But we have yet to tease out the essential connections uniting the body and the land.

Sexuality and the land both have a life of their own. The cycles of the land, determined by soil, weather, and biology, exist apart from the decisions of the farmer, just as we do not control the cycles of sexuality, which are governed by desire, fertility, and menstruation. The land embodies a particular geography, forcing the farmer to work creatively with hill, creek, and grove. Sexuality has its own geography, too; it determines our shape, breast, beard, and hip. It is ours, and not ours. Puberty is a painful recognition that there is within me a life that "goes on without me"—and gives me pimples. This is the otherness of both sexuality and the land. It is that which presents itself as primordially given.

The otherness of the land is greeted with enthusiasm by organic farmers and advocates of permaculture, a system of

farming that seeks to work with, rather than against, nature.
A new breed of philosophical farmer is interested in the
harmonious and sustainable use of the land as a rebuttal to
industrialized farm systems. The otherness of sexuality, on
the other hand, remains a source of suspicion. The moralizing
religious person and the medicalizing feminist are in agreement
here. Both see the otherness of sexuality as encroaching on
the person. The moralist sees sexuality as encroaching on the
life of the spirit, a separate demand of the sinful flesh and an
embarrassment to be repressed.
The advocate of contraception
and legalized abortion sees
the body's cycles and fertility
as encroaching on the life of
work and fulfillment, a separate
demand of biology and an
inconvenience to be repressed.
The former advocates fasting,
mortification, and prayer; the
latter—ethinylestradiol. Both

> CONTROL IS OUR
> METHOD OF MAKING
> THAT WHICH HAS ITS
> OWN LIFE ABSOLUTELY
> OURS, STRIPPED OF ALL
> OTHERNESS.

shudder in the face of a force within us that goes on without us,
quite without permission, a life that belongs to us, and yet—
terrible thought—we belong to it.

This is why the sexual revolution inaugurated an age of
control rather than an age of freedom. Control is our method
of making that which has its own life absolutely ours, stripped
of all otherness. The totalitarian state controls its subjects,
stripping from them the life that goes on apart from the state
by implementing instruments of power—secret police, spies,

propaganda. Modern sexual existence implements techniques of power—pornography, menstrual suppression, abortion, surgery—to strip sexuality of its otherness and render it absolutely subject to our desires. The logical tendency of sexual control really does aim toward this absolute. Transhumanists dream of "the end of sex" and "the inevitable rise of the artificial womb" (to quote two recent headlines), pining for an absolute control over pregnancy. The more enthusiastic advocates of contraception look to a future of total fertility control, where women will be semisterile, fertile only when they choose to be, through implants and IUDs. Everything that presents itself as given, as a possible surprise, will be reconfigured so it becomes the outcome of a willful decision. Every outcome can be traced to our rational choice. Nothing can be given.

If this all sounds wonderfully progressive, recall that the average sexual life fits somewhere on a scale of "stressful" to "unendurably frustrating," that many women appear to be less satisfied and happy after the sexual revolution than before. The price of transmutating our dominant relationship with our sexuality has been, paradoxically, an increased dependence on structures of power to maintain this control. The independence that contraception, sterilization, and abortion give us from our fertility is achieved by a simultaneous dependence upon pharmaceutical companies, surgeons, and abortionists. The independence pornography gives our sexual arousal from actual encounters with another is achieved by an increased dependence on the pornography industry, on its stars, producers, and slaves. The freedom the ever-growing system of gender theory gives us from binary sexual identities is bought at the price of a dependence on academics to define and distinguish between the pansexual from the omnisexual, the nonsexual from the asexual, the biromantic or the two-spirited from the polyamorous and bisexual. The freedom of divorce is a dependence on the legal system, and the independence surgery gives us from our bodies is simultaneously a dependence on surgeons—and the means to pay them.

Every liberating innovation in the erotic sphere has brought with it a chain of increased dependence on the impersonal structures of power behind it. The will to power has made us powerless. It is the poor, who cannot afford many of the expert services and technologies required to dominate our sexuality, who most suffer the consequences of a culture of sexual dependency.

Then how are we to live? With an eye on agriculture. It would be absurd if the farmer took the same tack of stark dominion, saying: "This land that belongs to me has a life of its own. I will control that life and thereby be the sole master of my property. I will no longer be a slave to its ecology. My power will be the sole source of its fruits." No. It is obvious that the otherness of the land is precisely what enables the farmer to farm. The farmer places his seeds in soil he did not create, under the sun he cannot command. He uses what is given, and only because it is "already going on" can he use it at all. He works in cooperation with the land, not by sheer mastery over it. Even the most technological agricultural practices rely, at base, on processes beyond the farmer's control. Planting crops without rotating them, plowing without regard to the particulars of geography, these efforts abase the unique life of nature, forcing it to comply with the monochrome will of man. They are idiotic efforts that end in dust bowls. It is the unique life of the land that enables us to use it in the first place. Unsustainable use does not respect the otherness of that which is used. It is a phenomenon of hypercontrol, one that denies the life that goes on apart from our power and desire.

The unsustainable use of our sexuality is really the destruction of the grounds for our enjoyment of it in the first place. It is precisely the otherness of sexual arousal, for instance, that makes it enjoyable, the fact that the body responds to another without asking permission. This is the adventure, surprise, and danger of erotic feeling. It can neither be forced nor summoned up by the sheer power of choice, but comes as a blessing and a gift. The indulgence of

THE UNSUSTAINABLE USE OF OUR SEXUALITY IS REALLY THE DESTRUCTION OF THE GROUNDS FOR OUR ENJOYMENT OF IT IN THE FIRST PLACE.

pornography and masturbation makes erotic feeling and sexual pleasure the outcome of our willful decision. It is always chosen, done to oneself, administered in a controlled time and place, with total power over its indulgence, and actively opposed to the other-orientated nature of sexuality. With the advent of internet pornography, our power to control attains a new height. We sit before an infinite array of possible stimuli. A real person cannot compete with pornography, not because he or she lacks this or that arousing trait, but because a real person is an *other*, a unique private life. A real person checks our growing desire for control by asserting, like the land, a unique life of his or her own.

Our sexuality cannot sustain being reduced to our total control any more than the soil can sustain a single high-yield crop. More and more evidence points to the conclusion that addiction and erectile dysfunction, not some wild freedom, are the fruits of male pornography use. Pornography becomes boring, pleasure decreases, and the capacity for sexual activity is diminished because we have destroyed the very means by which pornography was pleasurable in the first place—responding powerfully to something other than ourselves.

A SUSTAINABLE SEXUAL EXISTENCE RESPECTS THE OTHERNESS OF SEXUALITY.

No matter how much a farmer may wish to grow a single crop, he knows the soil will be harmed by it, and the very possibility of future growth will be ruined, so he plants in harmony with the life that goes on without him, rotating his crops. He does not see the land as a mere extension of his will, but as embodying a life of its own.

A sustainable sexual existence respects the otherness of sexuality. It is not merely an extension of our power. It goes on without us, intimately bound up with other people, with the given—the body we did not ask for, the kiss we do not deserve, the child we cannot will into or out of being. Control (from *contra*, "against") opposes the otherness of what is used, and thus cannot be the foundation for a happy sexual existence, which is a phenomenon of otherness. A new method of cooperation and harmony is needed.

To operate in harmony with our sexuality is not to succumb to its unique life. Yielding to every sexual drive is simply another way of destroying the otherness of sexuality. If by rigid control we destroy the otherness of sexuality and make it synonymous with our own power by succumbing to every sexual feeling and drive, we make ourselves synonymous with our sexuality. In both cases, diversity is reduced to identity, and the possibility of harmony is destroyed by the pretense that there is only one note playing. Instead of a marriage of body and soul, in which the partners celebrate a real unity without abasing their autonomy, we advocate on the one hand an angelism, in which the human spirit rules the body as a tyrant rules a rebel, and on the other a bestialism, in which the life of the body crushes the freedom of the soul.

What is needed is a sustainable attitude toward sexuality that respects its otherness without merely succumbing to it. If our body presents itself as a difficulty, our impulse should not be one of power, the eradication of that difficulty, but a cooperation with the body along with its difficulties, that we might sustain and not destroy. It is not by accident that Pope Francis, in his encyclical *Laudato Si'*, connected sexuality and the land, arguing that "thinking that we enjoy absolute power over our own bodies turns, often subtly, into thinking that we enjoy absolute power over creation. Learning to accept our body, to care for it and to respect its fullest meaning, is an essential element of any genuine human ecology."

There is an intimate connection between the fact that

something is other to us and that it is embedded in an ecosystem. An ecosystem is the complex network of an organism in relation to its environment. Taken in a broader sense, we consider a thing as embedded in an ecosystem when we contemplate the multitude of relations that make it up. This consideration is at the same time a recognition of the otherness of the thing. How clear this is in our encounters with other people! What makes our friend stand out as "his own" or "her own" more than contemplating his multitude of relations, that she grew up under the eye of a particular father, that his grandmother means the world to him, that she struggles to relate to her sister, that he mourns the death of his brother? Precisely by seeing a person as part of an ecosystem that exceeds our knowledge, as a center of a history and a narrative made up of relations that will never be ours, we begin to see our friend as "other" to us.

The whole work of ecology is to mark out the web of relations in which all things are embedded, especially those relations that exceed our power and particular ends. The fish is not just our food—it is the bear's and the eagle's; it is a filter of water and itself a feeder, supplying this tribe with a ritual and that city with food. To respect a thing in accordance with its multitude of relations, those known and unknown, is to respect a thing as other, with a life of its own—an existence that affects and is affected quite apart from our designs. All unsustainable use disregards a thing as existing in relation to other things.

We are shocked to learn that condoms, by reducing female exposure to the prostaglandins contained in male semen, may reduce the bonding effect of sexual intercourse; but this is only because we deny that sexuality is embedded in a relationship with human bonding as much as with human pleasure and procreation. We resist any studies that posit a link between oral contraceptives and blood clotting, but this is only because we do not consider sexuality ecologically, fundamentally related to a total system, embracing the cardiovascular system as much as the mammary glands. Instead, the scope and breadth of sexuality is limited to the end we most desire to control—our fertility. That oral contraceptives have been shown to alter a woman's attraction to "genetically compatible" men, that, when using hormonal contraception, women in relationships "reported significantly lower levels of intrasexual competition"—these strange and fascinating connections should be no surprise to one who strives for sustainability, taking sexuality as it offers itself, embedded in a multitude of relations that go on without us.

I DO NOT MEAN TO LIMIT THIS ANTI-ECOLOGICAL PHENOMENON TO OUR USE OF CONTRACEPTION, THOUGH IT IS EASIER TO POINT OUT.

I do not mean to limit this anti-ecological phenomenon to our use of contraception, though it is easier to point out. It is present in pornography, which tends to reduce our sexual existence to enjoying only the comfort and pleasure of the sexual drive. It is present in divorce, whose ecological relations to economy, culture, and child psychology are still being drawn out. It is present in abortion, hookup culture, and artificial reproductive technologies. Should we be offended that our sexual life exceeds our direct control by branching out into diverse relations, those known and unknown? No more than the farmer should be offended that the land is embedded in a web of relations, which it is his task to learn and sustain, not merely for the good of the land, but for his own good and success as a farmer.

To live in harmony with our sexuality, (as opposed to using sexuality for ends that limit, control, and deny its total reality) is to live a more holistic, integrated existence. The project of sustainability is difficult precisely because it requires a deep understanding of what we use, an attitude of care and respect toward its unique life, and a willingness to deny ourselves and our immediate desires in favor of a greater good—the total integration of our sexuality with our person. A joy rises amid this difficulty. Just as democratic harmony puts an end to any temptation toward control and mastery in the state, the harmony of the person with his or her sexual existence inaugurates a season of personal freedom and the end of mere control.

Becoming Catholic

THE DIVINE ASCENT OF THE CHURCH LADY

I know the old ladies forever praying rosaries at the back of the church don't *really* live in the sacristy. I know the women who eternally surround the Mary statue didn't come with a "Buy Our Statue, Get an Aging Filipino!" deal. I know that the "Church lady" is a person like the rest of us, chock-full of her own doubts and insecurities. Yet the Church lady is also a type, just like the hero, celebrity, or the starving artist. I want to investigate this creature.

To really *live* in a place is to cease considering that place as a theoretical object detached from our experience, a "point on a map," an "apartment," "bungalow," or some other repeatable structure. When we live in a place, we saturate it with our experience, making it inseparable from the joys and sorrows of life, until we are unable to reduce the place back into just a building or one house among many. We make the house our home, wrapped up in our being. While it's a joke, it's a true joke. The Church lady lives in the Church, for to "live in the Church" isn't simply to spend a lot of time within its physical structure. There are janitors, youth ministers, and even religious who, putting in equal hours, will never amount to the exemplary status of the Church lady. You and I enter our houses of the holy in spurts, bursting open the doors in moments of crisis or lighting candles in weeks of enthusiasm. The Church lady observes these interruptions from the back pew where, wrapping up her 900-day novena to St. Gertrude, she prays for our sorry souls.

The constant geographical presence of the Church lady is a physical manifestation of a spiritual presence to the Divine, one that reeks of audacious familiarity, unrepentant companionship, and a confident *being-with* the Lord, a being-with that has ceased to consider his house as some extrinsic, conceptual place, and has begun to consider it as home. The Church is inseparable from her being. She cannot reduce it back to a theoretical object, an institution she may or may not devote herself to, or a possible place in a world of possible places.

THE CHURCH LADY IS IMPOSSIBLY BAD AT ENTERTAINING POSITIONS OUTSIDE OF THE CHURCH.

This becomes obvious when we consider how easily the "Christian of the world" is embarrassed by the Church lady. A young man tells a Church lady he is an atheist. She responds, in all earnestness: "Talk to God about it." Another says, with the papal superiority of a *Catholic Reporter* reader, that the practice of praying to the saints is a decadent, merit-based, medieval disruption of the early Church's pure concept of Unity in Christ. She says: "Pray to St. Thomas, he's the patron saint of skeptics." Another tells her that he doubts the Real Presence. She responds: "He's used to it."

The Church lady is impossibly bad at entertaining positions outside of the Church, even for the sake of argument. She argues from the Church. God is so far from being a theory or a topic of debate that he cannot be held in suspense or treated as if nonexistent. Such a position might work for the concept *God*, a God extrinsic to my being, a God "out there" who I may affirm or deny. It doesn't work for the God who lives with us, who speaks to us, who cares for us. It's as if one were to say "I don't believe in the existence of your husband." The husband is so real, so suffered, so lived-with, that it would hardly occur to us to respond from this idea of his nonexistence. We would hardly begin by arguing, "Well, if my husband didn't exist, who's gin am I buying?" We'd assert the obvious daily experience of his existence: "Of course he exists, go talk to the fool yourself!"

This is the critical method of the Church lady, for whom Church is home and God is companion. She suffers the divine, lives with it, eats it, and as a result, seems foolish in our secular age, for whom the divine is an *option*, but never a *given*—a possibility among other possibilities, never simply *lived with* beyond doubt.

We look for heroes of apophatic mysticism in the caves of ascetics. We should be looking to the ladies at the Divine Mercy Chaplet. The transcendence of our concepts of God does not result in a speechless encounter with the One, a stripping away of all our profane knowledge until we are left with an awe in the face of "that of whom nothing can be said." Those are still concepts anyways, the concept of "that of which nothing can be said," the concept of "the One." We trade in our all-too-human ideas of God, not for an inhuman idea, but for a relationship *with* God. We know God as we know our friends: by transcending all that can be said *about* them and entering into a sphere in which we actively relate *to* them—loving them, speaking to them, consoling them.

The atheist is told to talk to God about his atheism because the Church lady is unwilling to take his stance and consider God as an object, a possible, and a theory available to affirmation and denial. She lives in and with the reality of God, and asserts it foolishly. She is always at Church and she refuses to leave, even for the sake of a suave apologetic. This is the price for really believing. It becomes harder to entertain the skeptical proposition to build a proof of the Creator, harder to intellectually suspend our certainty of God's existence. As we ascend the divine ladder to Church-lady status, we become more likely to proclaim than argue, more likely to shout, "He is risen" than consider the question of the Resurrection according to the discipline of the academic historians. We are in love, and it's easier to doubt my own existence than that of the beloved, making it that much harder to argue from the blank space of modern secularism, in which God's existence is hung perpetually in doubt.

The Church needs to give reason for its hope, coherent testimony to the Sacred in a secular age, but a love of reasonable argument that leaves behind the validity and efficacy of the Church lady is unreasonable. When God is suffered rather than merely believed in, we become foolish, but it's holy tomfoolery, evangelically cunning beyond all attempts at cunning. She makes no arguments, or she makes bad arguments, but only because she already is an argument. May she live forever.

HOW TO PRAY BADLY

I cannot comprehend the fact of the saint. I shudder and grind to a halt when contemplating the contemplators because I can't help but think one must get so tired of it all. At the end of the day surely there are only so many *Ave Marias* one can mutter. Surely it's extremism to live a life in constant prayer, constant mortification, and *constant* contemplation of Christ. Surely, in short, the saints get bored of sainthood.

We've all been there, when the prayer on our lips curls up and dies like a spider; when the faith that surrounds us bores; when Mass is a chore, fasting a pain, and obedience to the Church frightfully difficult. (I am usually made aware of this sad fact when halfway through the third mystery of the Rosary I realize I've spent thirty-five Hail Marys thinking about bacon.)

But the Saints hold a terrifying secret. It is the answer to the uncomprehending modern and the mediocre Catholic. It is the reason for their small smiles in their portraits; it is the reason their eyes burn like hearths within them. They have no idea what they're doing. None at all. (Now I hear the battle cry of Thomists rising slowly from their desks, so I run swiftly to my explanation.)

Saints are not people who have done a thing so many times they are good at it and rewarded appropriately. They are not experts, as we might call the top scientist in a field, nor are they winners. We would not say of saints, "They are good at what they do." Saints repeat and repeat and repeat again the spiritual life, not to become good at it, but to become bad at it. (Bear with me, the Thomists have been joined by herds of Benedictine nuns, and they are streaming down the hill, enraged goats charging the library where I write.)

SAINTS REPEAT AND REPEAT AND REPEAT AGAIN THE SPIRITUAL LIFE, NOT TO BECOME GOOD AT IT, BUT TO BECOME BAD AT IT.

When you repeat a word again and again, the word becomes strange on your tongue. Who invented such an obnoxious mouthful as "toast"? What is "toast"? Toast, toast, toast, toast. It's this strange, wet tap on the roof of the mouth, a stupid slackening of my jaw and tightening of the cheeks, then an entire reformation of the organ into an evil grin that pushes out a hiss of air, ending in that same odd slap of tongue. I have no idea what "toast" is now, but when I reestablish it with slightly burnt bread, it's a newfound delight. What a marvel, that that awkward mouthful means this crunchy, peanut-butter-coated mouthful.

Or take our fathers. We see them every day until they kick us out of the house and beg that we find gainful employment. We think, surely, this is one of the men I know best. But then you experience this moment, speaking to your father, looking at his face, when suddenly the who-you-think-he-is falls away and you realize you don't know in the least this giant individual who runs your house. Who is this man? I've been hugging him on a daily basis, thinking nothing more of it than it is that-which-I-do, but he was born of some woman, he grew up and kissed girls and had religious experiences, got drunk for the first time and all the times after that—why, he hugged a larger man on a daily basis! My God, who is this creature?

And again, when we reestablish this strangeness with the idea of Father, what a powerful view we are granted of fatherhood! Here is a man, in all his mystery, who has raised me and protected me from my youth—what a man.

The constant prayer of the saints is not an effort to become good at praying but a fiery effort to pray for the first time. To speak the words, "My God I believe, I adore, I trust, and I love thee," in somewhat of the same manner we spoke toast, to utter them as they are incredible, virgin, foreign. To pray well is to pray badly, to allow the words to shock us as strange, to permit the well-worn phrases to be things we can scarcely comprehend, to cave in to those names of Christ—Wonderful Counselor, Prince of Peace—to let them be names that strike us rudely, not mere names we project for a lifetime onto the Savior. To pray constantly is to seek that shining moment of praying as awfully as a child. Repetition is the preparation of the heart for the revelation that God is always new, never exhausted—the coolness of a pillow that never grows warm.

The saint gazing at an icon of Christ does not gaze to gaze well. He gazes to confirm the suspicion that he cannot understand it at all. He gazes for hours to see the face of Christ for one second. He contemplates for years to realize that he has not enough lifetimes to contemplate. The expert would seek an answer. The saint seeks a mystery. The expert would gaze well. The saint looks at the face of Christ like a child looks at a bird on his windowsill.

This Christianity of ours is dying. It is dying because we are seeing it for the 999th time. Its language has been destroyed. Think of the phrase our Evangelical-Protestant culture has gifted to the world. "Jesus Saves." This is entirely true, but it is entirely dead. As author Walker Percy says:

> *The Christian novelist is like a man who goes to a wild lonely place to discover the truth within himself and there after much ordeal and suffering meets an apostle who has the authority to tell him a great piece of news...He, the novelist, believes the news and runs back to the city to tell his countrymen, only to discover that the news has already been broadcast, that this news is in fact the weariest canned spot announcement on radio-TV, more commonplace than the Exxon commercial, that in fact he might just as well be shouting Exxon! Exxon! for all anyone pays attention to him.*

Jesus, save us from "Jesus Saves!" Everyone knows it for the 999th time, and no one knows it at all. But there is an answer. Our Lord speaks to us in the lives of the saints: It is up to you to move the universe toward the thousandth and the first experience of the truth. It is left to you to become saints, to see your God, your faith, and your world so awfully that it might be shocked with new life. Did you think I was lying when I told you you must become like little children? I was speaking the truth. Unless you are as wide-eyed and stunned by my grace as a child is by the first robin of Spring, you will not enter the Heavenly Kingdom.

Those Horribly Sappy Saints

Belief in the saints, properly understood, is a shocked assent to the fact that an ass like Ignatius, a self-abusing romantic like Francis, and a whore like Augustine all died loving God more than themselves. It's they who don't believe in the saints who demand the greatest saintliness of them. They imagine to have "exposed" the saint by pointing out some error, hatred, or insanity glossed over by the hagiographers. But it's an odd sort of exposé, and one the Christian tends to enjoy. It's because the saints are so obviously flawed that Christians—ignorant, hateful, and crazed, all—have hope of sharing in their everlasting joy.

This principle, in which the exposé of Christianity unwittingly becomes its defense, is apparent in the critique of the sentimentality of the saints. Two classic examples recommend themselves: Nietzsche fires a sick burn some thousand years backward to lambaste St. Augustine as a whining, adolescent girl, and William James, in his *The Varieties of Religious Experience*, says that St. Thérèse's "idea of religion seems to have been that of an endless amatory flirtation." Their idea—equally present in the stern, Reformation critique of Catholic effeminacy—is that sappiness is a sure sign of something rotten and false in a spirituality.

Obviously there is no need to defend a saccharine sentimentality when it rears it cloying head. Acknowledging that a human being kicked the bucket with some modicum of spiritual perfection does not require us to enjoy her diary entries. Asking for the speedy help of St. Bonaventure hardly means I have to pray, with him, that "my whole soul may ever languish and faint for love"—a Popsicle in the divine microwave.

I FEEL AWKWARD READING LUISA PICCARRETA REFER TO THE MOTHER OF GOD AS "MAMA."

I, for one, feel awkward reading Luisa Piccarreta refer to the Mother of God as "Mama." I marvel that Sr. Faustina can make such a metaphysically intimidating diary entry as, "I have come to understand His Trinitarian Quality and the Absolute Oneness of His Being," only to follow it with, "I want to be a quiet little dwelling place for Jesus to rest in. I shall admit nothing that might awaken my Beloved." From these I flee to a spiritual kinship with author and essayist Flannery O'Connor. She writes: "I hate to say most of these prayers written by saints-in-an-emotional state. You feel you are wearing somebody else's finery and I can never describe my heart as 'burning' to the Lord (who knows better) without snickering."

But before we do away with sappiness, consider the wit of our dear philosopher G.K. Chesterton, who said: "It is a good sign in a nation when things are done badly. It shows that all the people are doing them. And it is bad sign in a nation when such things are done very well, for it shows that only a few experts and eccentrics are doing them, and that the nation is merely looking on." It is not plainly and simply bad that the saints are sappy. Rather, it is exactly the type of badness we would expect from a genuinely personal relationship.

If God really is a person and the relationship of his creatures to himself is one of love, then he is the inevitable object of silly sentimentality. First, he exposes himself to our development. Who would not blush to read the professions of love they wrote in middle school? Who could bear to hear the self-absorbed, cliched claims to devotion they burbled out over the course of freshman romance? There is something eminently human about a gradual honing of feeling and its expression. A professional, even-tempered, and articulate middle-school romance is a contradiction in terms. If God really is a person, and if his desire is a relationship of love, then we should expect some of those persons who really encounter him to undergo a development of affection as much as they would in any love relationship.

Secondly, God as person exposes himself to the logic of personal intimacy. Being in love means becoming incomprehensible to the world. It is the life-affirming cocreation of a new and private country with its own borders, geography, and language. The awkwardness we feel when we overhear some sappy remark between lovers—some "coochy coo" or "honey bun"—may be a justified disgust at an infantile romance, but it may also be recognition of a world that we have no part in, a world only properly comprehensible to those within it, a world with its own greetings, jokes, and names. The lack of incomprehensible and awkward behaviors would be a sure sign that the saint has some other god than God at the receiving end of his or her adoration—the Moral Law, perhaps, or the Noble Ideal, but certainly not an actual someone with whom one whispers, jokes, and laughs.

If God had revealed himself as the Necessary, Unmoved Spirit who began the Universe, then the desire for an unsentimental gratitude toward the divine Cause would make sense. If God revealed himself as the Moral Law, then I might sympathize with the assessment of John W. Robbins, who, in his essay "The Church Effeminate," rejoiced that the "Reformation Church substantially purged Christianity of its feminine elements, leaving men and women alike faced with a starkly masculine God, in which true faith is energetic, active, steadfast, mighty, industrious, powerful."

Certainly, there are evangelical benefits to the true faith being an industrial faith, never ridiculous, hapless, bungling, silly, or sappy. The Church would go a long way with CEOs. But by making God the object of our seriousness—banning the possibility of false sentiment, infantile sentiment, incomprehensible intimacy, and all those dubious and earnest odors of sanctity—we ignore God as he reveals himself in Scripture. He is a Trinity of persons, eminently concerned with our particular life, who desires a relationship and initiates and makes this relationship possible in the person of Jesus Christ— even at the risk of looking like a fool.

So let the stoics sneer at a faith flecked through with languishing souls and awkward devotions. Let the aesthetes turn their noses at the ugly holy cards and plaster statues.

For my part, I deny the possibility of a genuine faith unless it simultaneously has the capacity for awkward, incomprehensible, infantile, idiotic, and sappy moments with the Great God of Wrath.

The Difference Between an Idiotic and an Ecstatic Hierarchy

I t is difficult to defend the fact of hierarchy as crucial to attaining the good proper to human beings. The word has positive origins—an "order of angels"—but its usage in our disenchanted age indicates no more than an ordering of highest to lowest in a given system, or in the case of popular conscience, a secretive pyramid scheme. This distaste is not entirely unfounded. Our typical experience of hierarchy is one of oppression and corruption, whether in corporations (in which the wage slavery of the lower serves the profits of the higher) or in bureaucracies (in which the lower suffers for the mistakes of the higher).

It is difficult, then, to be Catholic. To grow in the pedagogy of the Catholic Church is to grow in and through a hierarchy. Whether it's displayed in its sheer aesthetic form in the "kiss of peace" passed from priest, to deacon, to subdeacon, to altar servers during the Tridentine Mass or in the order of authority from Pope to Bishop to Priest, the nuances of which any child growing up in Bible Belt America must memorize in order to wrestle with the Protestants, hierarchy is everywhere.

With obvious instances of corruption chewing at the Church hierarchy it becomes paramount for any Catholic who wishes to retain his faith to develop a philosophy of hierarchy or to investigate the claims of hierarchy against a world grown bitter to the very idea of it. Without a positive defense of the thing, Catholics are prone to an ecclesial Cartesianism, in which we make a distinction between the Real Church (a purely spiritual entity) and the Hierarchical Church (a purely historical accident). A properly Catholic understanding of hierarchy serves more purposes than retaining the unity and singularity of the Church—it describes the human person as a hierarchical being, and extends its importance beyond Church walls into every life as a crucial element of all human flourishing.

> TO GROW IN THE PEDAGOGY OF THE CATHOLIC CHURCH IS TO GROW IN AND THROUGH A HIERARCHY.

The idea is best explained negatively. If a hierarchy exists for a particular level of its total order (for the 1 percent, the bishops, or the boss) then it ceases to be hierarchy proper. It becomes a power structure. If hierarchy exists for an end beyond any one of its levels, then, and only then, does it deserve the fullness of the term hierarchy. We distinguish between two types of hierarchy, or between hierarchy and the power-structure which apes at hierarchy. The latter is an idiotic hierarchy (from *idios*, meaning "one's own"), a hierarchy turned in on itself, serving some particular class, while the former is an ecstatic hierarchy (from *exstasis*, to "stand outside of oneself"), and is directed toward an end beyond itself.

It's difficult to deny that an ecstatic hierarchy is something gloriously human. If I am building a house and someone with greater talent joins my effort, we will, quite naturally, establish a hierarchy. I will give up my attempts to perform complex masonry, occupy a lower-value skill set (mixing cement, say), and let my friend use his higher-value skill set. I would not resent my friend for taking a higher place, for the simple reason that our being so ordered best serves our common goal—the house will be built, and better. Our hierarchy is a hierarchy-for. We are a team.

It is a positive joy to find someone better than me when my desire is for some goal outside of myself. But the moment my desire is for my own satisfaction, comfort, or advancement, then the existence of a higher rank becomes an opportunity for resentment. My friend is no longer essential to achieving the goal of a well-built house, he is a competitor for individual happiness, earning a better wage and occupying a position that serves his individual needs better than my position serves my own. Here the existence of a higher negates the lower, where previously the existence of the higher served the common end of both the lower and the higher. Here the lower becomes useful only in the service of the higher, where previously both were useful in serving an end beyond themselves. The hierarchy has become idiotic, its members concerned with themselves rather than with that common goal that transcends its members.

Hierarchy, understood ecstatically, is beautiful. It is not something rudely imposed. It is a social order drawn out of human beings by their common vision of an end. It does not offend equality—all are equally oriented toward a common good. It does not offend diversity—it thrives on it, seeing the right arrangement of lower and higher as the most effective means of achieving an end that transcends the grasp of any one "level" within the hierarchy. Anyone who has been excited to be part of a team has experienced this feeling of hierarchy springing into place as a natural response of the human heart to a goal beyond itself.

This is the nature of Church hierarchy. It is fundamentally ordered to ends outside of itself—the worship of God, the salvation of souls, and the universal communion of all humanity in Christ. The ordering of higher and lower—bishops, priest, deacons, laity—is an effective means of attaining these ends. An antipathy between the "clergy" and the "laity" within the People of God is a sure sign we've forgotten what we're doing as the Church. We have forgotten the goal that transcends the lot of us and unifies us in diverse equality.

This notion of a common goal that orders a human community into higher and lower is fundamentally opposed to a Marxist dialectic which posits an unavoidable class warfare culminating in the abolition of class—in a unity gained, not by reference to a common good in the light of which diversity in station is desirable, but by a leveling of diversity. The seminal social encyclical *Rerum Novarum* by Pope Leo XIII sounds naïve to modern ears when it says that the Church "tries to bind class to class in friendliness and good feeling," and that "mutual agreement [between classes] results in the beauty of good order," but the rejection of class warfare for class friendship follows from the Catholic view of hierarchy. Every level of a hierarchy is united in love for each other insofar as each level is seen as necessary for the attainment of a common, transcendent good.

It is not in spite of, but through its hierarchical understanding of the universe that the Church simultaneously affirms a radical equality of dignity between class and class, person and person, layperson and cleric, and so on. The Church roots equality in the status of each person as a son or daughter of God. The Church describes this status as the destiny of humanity attained through adoption—the taking-in of humanity into the family of God through the person of Jesus Christ. The theological details need not be described here. Suffice to say that the orientation of humanity to a final transcendent goal—becoming family with God—orders humanity

THE SELFISHNESS OF CLERGYMEN HAS CREATED A CLIMATE OPPOSED TO HIERARCHY.

into an hierarchy and serves as a positive ground for universal human dignity, just as the goal of a well-built house orders workers into hierarchy while blessing them with the equality of a team.

The greater the transcendent goal, the more horrible it is to replace it with the goals of the immanent self. It makes sense that the selfishness of clergymen has created a climate opposed to hierarchy. But perhaps a reason we have a seemingly natural antipathy toward hierarchy (besides the mediocre examples of idiotic anti-hierarchies) is that we live a very recent and very dubious philosophy of individualism. A total critique would go beyond the scope of this essay, but there are two presuppositions of this philosophy that erect a wall against any healthy understanding of hierarchy.

First, the idea that we exist without definite purpose, making our own meaning, neither living up to nor failing to live up to our true self, but choosing who we are. All this makes being ordered to some definite purpose something extrinsic, foreign, and awkward to the human person. If we are those types of beings without definite purpose, then ecstatic hierarchy, which is by its nature purposeful, cannot be natural to us. It presents itself as something unessential and arbitrarily chosen.

> THE JOY WE TAKE
> IN HIERARCHICAL
> STRUCTURES IS
> NATURAL TO US AS
> FLOURISHING
> HUMAN BEINGS.

Secondly, the idea that the individual exists prior to community, rather than being constituted in and through communion (always already in relation to other people, already a son, already a daughter)—this, once again, makes hierarchy something extrinsic to humanity. If individuality is our true nature, then our natural orientation is not toward any common good or shared goal, but to our individual fulfillment and satisfaction. Hierarchy, in this view, ought to be an idiotic hierarchy—a group justified not by its common goal, but by its self-enclosed service to individual members. This, at least, is the view of American liberalism that grounds itself in the contract theory of human society, in which humanity gathers and consents to governance, not for any goal outside of the individual, but for the protection of every individual from the other.

When these highly Americanized ideas combine in a critique of the Church hierarchy, silliness results. The irony is that the resentful layperson and the corrupt bishop often join hands in a mutual presupposition—that hierarchy ought to be ordered to serve individuals. I resent the priest and rail against him hoarding the capacity to forgive sins or for limiting the priesthood to men because I believe the Church should be fundamentally ordered to my individual satisfaction, to the promotion of my rights, my fulfillment. I desire an equality of function between layperson and cleric because I am being denied what is owed to me. So too the bishop who lives in a mansion, takes the tithes, and otherwise oppresses the Church implicitly believes that the Church is ordered to his individual satisfaction, to the fulfillment of his desires. He desires no equality of function between layperson and cleric because he has limited the focus of an idiotic, inwardly turned hierarchy toward a particular class of individuals—if not simply himself. In both cases, ecstasy is abandoned for idiocy, and a transcendent goal is abandoned for self service.

But if the nature of humanity is ecstatic, if I become fully myself by transcending myself, by rising from the individual to the Family, from the egoistic "I" to the ecclesial "we," from the self to the other—then hierarchy is an art, a modus operandi of being human and a fulfillment of our nature. Mother Church becomes a school of love, not despite, but in her very hierarchical structure, ordering humanity away from egoism and toward a common good. The joy we take in hierarchical structures, whether in our childish delight for Pokemon or our adult appreciation for the well-ordered community, far from ousting us as a secret Fascist or an enemy of the Revolution, would be natural to us as flourishing human beings.

Religion and Changing the World

The older business generation criticizes my generation for a vague, objectless idealism. We want to "change the world," but we have no idea what we would like to change it into. We want to "make a difference"—though we are relatively inarticulate on the difference we would like to make. The criticism fits: we are hankering for some target to aim our rainbow rays of impact-making sentiment at. But the effort to locate the source of this problem in Disney movies and bad parenting misses the point.

Wanting to change the world is a fundamentally religious sentiment. My generation's idealism is not suffering from a lack of practical goals but from a lack of practical Christianity. We do not need the advice of a CEO troubled by millennial apathy in the workplace. We need a priest.

The philosopher Max Scheler argued that one cannot help but perform religious acts, a claim not proven, but certainly helped by the fact there has never been evidence of a historically irreligious culture. For instance, Scheler describes the act of worship as the act that places some value as the highest value, to which all others must be subordinated. Even the most hardened of atheists and the most cowardly of Christians have some highest value. All people, of all generations, worship, by the simple fact of being people who value things. The only question is what this value will be—life, erotic love, comfort, money, the State, the tribe, the family, and so on. The fascists knew this well, and worked diligently to make the State the object of worship. The millennial generation tends to make the self their highest value. The Middle Ages made God the highest priority.

The perception of the world as fallen and in need of resurrection is another one of these "religious acts." Almost without exception, every religion has some account of the Fall, whether the Original Sin of Judeo-Christianity, the fall into the "world of appearances" as described by the Hindus, Buddhists, and Neo-Platonists, the Greek and Roman myths of separation from the gods, and so on. The great religious historian Mircea Eliade would describe this as the primitive division of time into sacred time (pre-Fall) and profane time (post-Fall)—an "original act" of primitive man.

This perceptive act, by which one concludes there is a fly in the ointment, something broken or off about existence, is insufficient to explain our desire to change the world. The Stoics thought existence was a tragedy, but they would be much more interested in a man accepting his fate than making a difference. The Buddhist knows the world is suffering, but the movement of Buddhist instruction is not to "go out there and change the world" but to "go within and change yourself."

It is Judaism and, in a particularly sharp way, Christianity, that inaugurates the idea, the genuine possibility, of saving the world. They do this by declaring that all is not lost—a Messiah is coming who will fix the broken world. The "sacred time" will be restored. The Christian feels this like a knife because Christianity declares this world changer has come—God himself. Even more incredibly, God urges us to take part in this world-changing action. We are to make the broken world into the Kingdom of Heaven.

Millennials who vaguely want to "change the world" should appreciate that they are experiencing a uniquely post-Christian feeling. That they cannot articulate what they want to change the world into is because they have a Christian-act without any Christian-object, sentiment without belief, religious feeling without religion. It's not that the business leaders who criticize Millennials don't make this same religious act—they do—but

> **MILLENNIALS WHO VAGUELY WANT TO "CHANGE THE WORLD" SHOULD APPRECIATE THAT THEY ARE EXPERIENCING A UNIQUELY POST-CHRISTIAN FEELING.**

they position it as a matter of money. They describe the Fallen world as an economic problem redeemed by economic solutions. Millennials are too spiritual to pin the source of salvation on "smart capitalism," "economic innovation," and "leadership," but too materialistic to pin it on the Christ, and so they pin it nowhere in particular.

Jack Kerouac called his generation the Beatific or "Beat"

Generation, because he believed they would see God. My generation is the Lapsarian generation, because, while we have given up on seeing God, we cannot help but see the Fall. We believe the world is broken—we no longer believe in the rebellion, in the movement that makes it whole.

This makes us look like idiots to an older generation. They demand that we clarify what, precisely, is wrong, and what, precisely, the world ought to be changed into, and we can only say "everything is wrong" and "something must be done." We are shoved forward by the powerful push of a long tradition that demands, at every moment, that the world be radically transformed into the Kingdom of Heaven.

As the fascist makes the State his object of worship, as a Don Juan makes erotic experience his liturgy, or as the atheist seems to make the mysteries of space his outlet for religious wonder, so we, the nonreligious, recognize the Fall. We simply express it in terms of "The Problem." The Problem could be the communists, the Jews, or the homosexuals; the capitalist class or the bourgeois; the patriarchy, the government, or religion itself. The point is simply this—one thing is the reason, at least in sentiment, that the whole world is bust.

Calling some tangible thing "The Problem" seems more sensible than positing an Original Sin that implicates the entire human family in an evil-beset Cosmos. But press the person who says that "it's all gone to hell now that those [foreigners] are here," and you'll find that The Problem is not a practical, solvable one. It is an infinite one. There is always some Other who is The Problem. Today he may be the Jew, tomorrow the communist, and next week the Catholic. The finite object is infinitized. The Other takes the place of the Fall of Man. Press (certain) feminists and you'll find the "patriarchy," through which we have all the violence of the day, is either inextricably rooted in human psychology (*a la* Freud, Levi-Strauss, Lacan) or given some origin in a prepatriarchal Paradise unavailable to historical investigation. In both cases, the problem is not some finite, practical problem—it is The Problem. The nationalist must be eternally vigilant against the arrival of the Other. The feminist must continually fight against the patriarchy. One can no more solve The Problem than one can solve the sin of Adam and Eve.

THE PROBLEM IS NOT A PRACTICAL, SOLVABLE ONE. IT IS AN INFINITE ONE. THERE IS ALWAYS SOME OTHER WHO IS THE PROBLEM.

Many Marxists have the decency to make this explicit: the true Problem is the warfare of capital and labor within the dialect of production. Few still hope for a finite revolution that will establish the worker's paradise in Russia or Spain. The task has been spiritualized. One can fight from one's desk at a capitalistic-state funded university. One can share socialist memes on Facebook. The Revolution is an infinite effort.

Those in the corporate Silicon Valley class tend to root all problems in a lack of unity, solvable by infinitely greater forms of communication, ending in a never-quite-attained "global community." Queer theorists posit an obligatory heterosexuality, solved by a constant troubling of the gender binary. Capitalists, especially of the Ayn-Randian ilk, blame the communists and seek salvation in the free market. The New Atheists blame religion—which "poisons everything," as Christopher Hitchens puts it—and seek salvation in the equally all-consuming and open-ended saviors of Science, Reason, and Progress.

We are not losing our religion. We have found too much of it. The removal of the "quaint" religious answers to the problem of the Fall has not led us into a world in which problems and their solutions are finite, practical, and limited. The removal of the religious answer has made secular answers religious. Problems become The Problem. Solutions become Final Solutions. They must: to meet a perception of total brokenness, one must totalize this or that particular instance of brokenness, and thus totalize the solution. The only way to stop positing The Problem is to cease having the religious perception of a broken world.

> CHRISTIANITY STATES THERE IS ONE, INFINITE PROBLEM AND ONE, INFINITE SOLUTION.

Christianity does not infinitize a finite object. It does not make this or that molehill into the mountain of the Fall. Christianity states there is one, infinite problem and one, infinite solution. Sin is The Problem. It makes humanity infinitely guilty. Mercy is the solution. It makes humanity infinitely atoned for.

The brightness of this vision does not blind the Christian to the here-and-now—quite the opposite. It is the totalized world problem that tends to make us apathetic. Whether The Problem is class warfare, patriarchy, the Other, the government, climate change, the Liberals, the New World Order—it is out of our hands. It is too big for us. When we call climate change the ultimate problem facing our generation, we are freed—to do very little. When we recognize a beggar's poverty comes from the inevitable exploitation of labor by capital, we feel no burn to give him a buck. The Problem, after all, is not going to be solved by charity. One must fight the age-old War of the Classes by organizing, protesting, agitating. Do we do these things? No, or at least not now, because now we have to go to work, check Facebook, and so on.

The totalized finite problem puts us in the perfect position of never having to become radical. It is never so big that we need a Savior; always just big enough to assure us we can't save anything. A radical change of lifestyle would do nothing to prevent the warming Earth, the oppression of the poor, the globalist Jews, the hidden agenda of the Catholic Church, or whatever The Problem may be. So we do not change our lives.

Christians are not absolved from solving this-world problems. They are absolved from making this-world problems the object of his religious consciousness. This frees them to act. Because Christians believe the whole world is fallen and needs to be saved, they are freed from the exhaustion of believing the whole world is class warfare and needs an infinite revolution. That humanity sins and needs mercy saves Christians from the infinite effort of believing that maleness is constituted by a primal rejection of the female as "other," who then bears all oppression.

Problems are not The Problem and so problems can be solved. World salvation is for the Lord, and neighborhood salvation is for his people. "The poor you will always have with you," said Jesus. Thus his followers have it on divine guarantee: no worldly solution will solve the problem. Neither revolution, nor eugenics, nor innovative and compassionate capitalism will remove the poor. "The poor you will always have with you" and thus it is you who will always be responsible for the poor. God decrees it: you may not pawn off the problem onto a total, forthcoming solution. You must practice limited acts of particularized justice. You must give alms, pray, fast, feed the hungry, clothe the naked, harbor the harborless, visit the sick, ransom the captive, and bury the dead.

The darkness of Original Sin allows Christians to be light of heart about this or that unoriginal sin. The vastness of the heavenly vision allows the vision of a heavenly neighborhood— or at least a peaceful one—to remain small and attainable.

This is the great scandal of the popes toward the Marxists. They do not recommend the never-quite-attained utopia of the classless society. They describe the oppression of labor by capital, not as The Problem, but as a problem. The encyclical *Rerum Novarum* of Pope Leo XIII recommends "friendship between the classes." We can scoff at the papal solution. (Just be friends? How quaint.) But the real horror of Catholic teaching is that it is genuinely possible. A person with capital and a person who labors can love each other. They can recognize their mutual interdependence and establish a relationship of justice. "If Christian precepts prevail, the respective classes will not only be united in the bonds of friendship, but also in those of brotherly love." If this is the case, then there is no escape. You are obligated, at every moment, to solve the finite, particular problem of class warfare by particular works of justice.

Christianity limits the religious consciousness to genuinely religious objects. By this limitation, she gives her followers the world as a bucket of nonreligious problems with nonreligious solutions. Oh, would Christians act accordingly!